Eastern Regions

Edited by Annabel Cook

Young Writers
First published in Great Britain in 2004 by:
Young Writers
Remus House
Coltsfoot Drive
Peterborough
PE2 9JX
Telephone: 01733 890066
Website: www.youngwriters.co.uk

SB ISBN 1 84460 583 3

Foreword

Young Writers was established in 1991 and has been passionately devoted to the promotion of reading and writing in children and young adults ever since. The quest continues today. Young Writers remains as committed to engendering the fostering of burgeoning poetic and literary talent as ever.

This year's Young Writers competition has proven as vibrant and dynamic as ever and we are delighted to present a showcase of the best poetry from across the UK. Each poem has been carefully selected from a wealth of *Once Upon A Rhyme* entries before ultimately being published in this, our twelfth primary school poetry series.

Once again, we have been supremely impressed by the overall high quality of the entries we have received. The imagination, energy and creativity which has gone into each young writer's entry made choosing the best poems a challenging and often difficult but ultimately hugely rewarding task - the general high standard of the work submitted amply vindicating this opportunity to bring their poetry to a larger appreciative audience.

We sincerely hope you are pleased with our final selection and that you will enjoy *Once Upon A Rhyme Eastern Regions* for many years to come.

Contents

The Poems

The Young Man From Crete

There was a young man from Crete,
He always had to eat meat,
He ate a lamb chop,
He bought from a shop
And threw the bone to young Pete.

Ronnie Downey (9)
Aveley Primary School, Aveley

I Want Food

There was a young man from Crete,
He had nothing he could eat,
He went to see Bob,
To get a new job,
To work with his uncle Pete.

Jordan Blake (9)
Aveley Primary School, Aveley

Limerick

There was a young man from Crete,
I'm sure that his name was Pete,
He got out of bed
And called his mate Fred,
They arranged a time to meet.

Ashley Bedford (9)
Aveley Primary School, Aveley

The Love Poem

Love is beautiful in all different ways
As beautiful as a field of daisies
Even though love is unrequited
I still find my heart is lighted.

Michael Chapple (11)
Aveley Primary School, Aveley

Oliver Twist

Oliver strolled towards the rusty room,
Not knowing that it would seal his doom.
He gazed into the busy space,
Then a mysterious shadow came walking, walking, walking.
The mysterious man came walking right up to Oliver's face.

Bill Sykes stared into Oliver's eyes,
Wondering if he would ever tell lies.
Bill was wearing a black leather hat
And a pair of trousers with the texture of a fluffy cat.

Nancy, the confident, motherly lady,
Mothered young Oliver like he was her baby,
Then a healthy family took Oliver away
So Bill beat Nancy to force her to kidnap Oliver today.

Then Nancy decided to save Oliver's life
But Bill took hers away by using a knife,
Knife, knife, knife,
Bill killed her by using a knife.

The whole of the country were after Bill
Because he was involved in an illegal deal.
Bill tried his very best to escape
But he fell from the sky and Oliver was safe.

Tom Olliffe, Jack Beck (11) & Joe Scott
Aveley Primary School, Aveley

Limerick

There was a young man from Crete,
I'm sure that his short name was Pete.
He fell out of bed
And cracked his poor head,
Now he is under the sheet.

Tysian Wood (9)
Aveley Primary School, Aveley

Oliver Twist

Oliver ran through the night of gloom,
Then met Fagin who showed him up to his room.
He stared at all the boys standing gloomily there
When an unpleasant man came climbing, climbing, climbing.
An unpleasant man came climbing up the old oak stair.

Oliver thought of Nancy as his mother.
She was kind and beautiful like no other.
Nancy did not show any fear when Bill hit her round the ear,
Crying, crying, crying.
Nancy was crying when Bill hit her round the ear.

Bill took Oliver to do a job
But Oliver was taken in by a wealthy family called Hobb.
Back in the thief den Bill and Fagin worried.
They must catch Oliver
So down the market they hurried.

Bill told Oliver to swing across
Even though Oliver had been bitten by frost.
Oliver made it across the rickety bridge and smiled at Bill.
Bill climbed after but slipped on the ridge, ridge, ridge.
He slipped to his death on the crumbling ridge.

Sara Downey (11)
Aveley Primary School, Aveley

Motor Cars

From my city window way up high
I like to watch the cars go by.
They look like burnished beetles, black,
That leave a little, muddy track
Behind them as they slowly crawl,
Sometimes they do not move at all
But huddle close with hum and drone
As though they feared to be alone.
They grope their way through fog at night
With the golden feelers of their light.

Jordan Richardson (10)
Aveley Primary School, Aveley

The Mole

As the ball flies through the air
the crowds turn and begin to stare.
Crash-landing on the green
the crowds sigh, 'Oh, what a scene.'

As I go to putt the ball
the crowds turn and begin to call.
Slowly the ball drops in the hole
there on the pole is a mole.

So from that day on
they call me the mole
who got the ball
in the first hole.

So that's how I got my name!

Scott Tony Rixson (11)
Aveley Primary School, Aveley

Daydreaming Dogs

Running and jumping
Howling and barking
Panting and snorting
Inside the small house munching and crunching
Gobbling and gulping
Her white and black tail swishing
Darting down the long garden
Beside the old vines which are crashing and creaking
Jumping and wondering
Would I be home ready for tea?

Sian Ayers (10)
Aveley Primary School, Aveley

It Wasn't Me, Miss!

It wasn't me, Miss!
It was her,
She dared me to do it.
I'm terrible but it wasn't me, Miss!
It was the girl with brown hair.

Please don't make everyone stare
But it wasn't me, Miss!
It was the girl with brown hair.
It wasn't me with the notebook who took all your pens
And it wasn't me who let out the hens.

It wasn't me in the girls' dens.
Please forgive me but it was her.
I'll tell you who it is
But you won't believe me.
It was the girl with brown hair.

Hollie Gowdy (10)
Aveley Primary School, Aveley

My Ball

My ball is
black and white
I boot it up high
into the sky.

I go to see
the summer season
and then I see
the ball again.

Sometimes I sit and wonder
why?
I see the mystic train
toot by.

Bradley Joseph Caudwell Sims (9)
Aveley Primary School, Aveley

I'd Rather . . .

I'd rather get chickenpox
I'd rather run ten miles
I'd rather the clock have a tock
Than do my homework piles.

I'd rather lose my pocket money
I'd rather bitten by a Staff
I'd rather talk till I am 99
Than kiss Aunty Kath.

I'd rather sail the Atlantic
I'd rather swim in a freezing pool
I'd rather do most any of these
Than find out that I'm not cool!

Perry Clout (9)
Aveley Primary School, Aveley

My Friendly Sticker

My happy sticker
Sits and waits for me at home
Smiling at me there.

It sits there all day
Will it ever go away?
Please don't go away.

You are my best friend!
I will take you everywhere
If you want to come.

Kelsie Donovan (10)
Aveley Primary School, Aveley

I'd Rather . . .

I'd rather do the housework
I'd rather clean my room
I'd rather do my homework
Than go up to the moon.

I'd rather wash the car
I'd rather smell stinky feet
I'd rather wash the dishes
Instead of eating meat!

Alice Rogers (8)
Aveley Primary School, Aveley

A Pocket Full of Rhyme

Giants are so high
I don't know why
Giants are so high
Perhaps they cry.
Giants are so high
They reach the sky.
Giants are so high
They have to die.
Giants.

Ben Wilson (10)
Aveley Primary School, Aveley

My Shetland

My Shetland white
Like a piece of snow
She is cuddly like a teddy bear
She kicks so high
She touches the sky
And kicks those cold and fluffy clouds away.

Scott Feltham (10)
Aveley Primary School, Aveley

Tiny

My little kitten, black and white,
7 months old and shines like a light.
She is timid and hides
And runs under our sides.
When she goes out to play
She always runs away.
She is black and white
And a pretty sight.
Her name is Tiny
And that's about right.

Toni Ann Kneller (11)
Aveley Primary School, Aveley

Rugby

I dream I am a famous rugby player.
My fingers tinkle in my heart.
Can I do it?
Heart pounding in my chest.
I wear white and a red rose.
Running down the wing.
Wait for the ball.
Do you know what team I am?
It's England, the champions of them all.

Luke Mainhood (9)
Aveley Primary School, Aveley

The Sunset In The Bathroom

It looks like a giant orange in the bath
The bright cloud as white as a bathroom ceiling
After a while it goes down, down, down
The sun is fun
A shot of a gun
That's why the sun is so, so fun.

Charmaine Cooper (10)
Aveley Primary School, Aveley

I Dream I Am A Famous Football Player

I dream I am a famous football player
Who plays for a united club
My kit is claret and blue
Which keeps me scoring through and through.
Each week I am on the football field
Instead of being sub
They are West London based
And we like to tour
When a million fans come to scream.
Can you guess who I wish to play for?
It's West Ham, of course.
The *supreme team!*

Christopher Benjamin Livermore (11)
Aveley Primary School, Aveley

The Girl With Brown Hair

The girl I adore has lovely brown hair
and light blue eyes.
She is the light of the school
to me, anyway.
She may be a year or two younger
but I do not care.
She is the light of the school
to me, anyway.
She likes expensive shoes and dresses.
She is the light of the school
to me, anyway.

James Oliver Brown (10)
Aveley Primary School, Aveley

Oliver Twist

Oliver walked through the dark, scary night.
He then entered Fagin's place, he was sure it was full of fright.
He slept there until the bright, sunny morning.
He was told that where he stayed was a thief den,
That was his first warning.

Then came Nancy and Bill looking cheerful.
She was attractive but he looked fearful.
Nancy loved the evil Bill.
Oh, how could she have the will?

Nancy cared for Oliver so well
But he ran away, was he going to Hell?
Nancy was beaten up by Bill
To make her kidnap Oliver in the chill.

Nancy helped Oliver to get away
But Bill killed her in the month of May.
Bill tried to escape on a rickety bridge
But fell to his death on a crumbling ridge.

Adam Osariase-Osifo (10)
Aveley Primary School, Aveley

Ham And Jam

I went to the shops to get some ham
but then I realised I needed some jam.
When I got home the fridge was full
with ham and jam.

After a while I was feeling hungry
so then I said I will have a ham and jam sandwich
but then I realised I needed some bread
so I went to the shops to get some bread
and when I got home I had a ham and jam sandwich.

Carly Robyn Milbourn (10)
Aveley Primary School, Aveley

Oliver Twist

Oliver walked cautiously through a dark patch of gloom
When he entered the crowded room that was to seal his doom
He glared at the hustle and bustle out there
Then storming, storming
A treacherous man came storming up the old, creaky stair.

Up came a woman, Nancy was her name
She was Bill's girlfriend, oh, what a shame
Nancy helped look after the boys
But they made such a noise.

Oliver tried to escape with Nancy's help
But Bill made her die with a piercing yelp!
Off Bill ran to catch Oliver now
Maybe he could grab him, but how?

They climbed up the derelict barn, no turning back
Bill stood on a tack as sharp as a knife
Oliver was frightened, he could not help
He turned and froze, then Bill frowned
He slipped and drowned
Bill frowned and finally slipped and drowned.

Jamie-Lee Gleed (10)
Aveley Primary School, Aveley

Jumbled John

I collapsed on the door and
I opened the couch.
I lazed on the TV and
I switched about.

I zoomed Mum if I was allowed to go out and
I asked out of the door and
Without hesitating I ran about.
I'm all scrambled up since I slipped on the floor.

Luke Fishwick (11)
Aveley Primary School, Aveley

Hunting Daniel

Barking and fighting
Running and walking
Snoring and roaring
On the bed, boiling and drooling
Biting and jumping
His back shining
And sniffing while meddling.

On the floor drinking and eating
Nibbling and growling
An animal of movement.

Danny Kerridge (10)
Aveley Primary School, Aveley

A Man From Peru

There was a man from Peru
Who dreamt he was eating his shoe.
He woke up in the night
With a big fright
And found his dream had come true.

Matthew Sibley (10)
Aveley Primary School, Aveley

Bedroom Blues

I fed this bright morning and
I staggered my fish
I gobbled down my stairs
And ate into the living room.

I lazed on the television
I chewed up my stairs
I'm all scrambled up since
I fell out of bed!

Bradley Howes (10)
Aveley Primary School, Aveley

Darting Daniel

Darting and dodging
Leaping and sprinting
Crashing and pouncing
Isn't that the house of darting and roaring?
Sneaking and crawling
With him roaring and growling
Laying down scratching
Above the level of running and panting
He's dribbling for food.

Conner Rowland (10)
Aveley Primary School, Aveley

Anyone Out There?

I am going now . . .

A cold breeze swishes past me
Making my skin shiver.

Sitting all alone
I've realised it's Saturday.
Tomorrow he comes.

Chelsea Drum (10)
Aveley Primary School, Aveley

The Work Book

The book fell over,
I have to pick it up quick,
before my boss comes.
it is his work book,
with all the work planned for me.
I open the book . . .
but it's all filled up
with loose papers and markings.
I hear the door squeak.

Lewis Rowell (11)
Aveley Primary School, Aveley

Oliver Twist

Oliver walked through a dark, jet-black gloom
when he entered the dusty, dull room that was to seal his doom.
He gazed at the hustle and bustle there.
A treacherous man came walking, walking, walking
a treacherous man came walking up the concrete stair.

He had a small, black hat,
standing next to a lady on a mat.
The man looked at Oliver in despair,
the lady came walking, walking, walking,
the lady came walking with long, ginger hair.

The lady was called Nancy
and Bill took a fancy.
Bill set a trap for Oliver Twist,
Bill rode hastily into the mist.

Inside there was a wall where Fagin put his gold,
all he wanted to do was keep it to hold.
Nancy had to do the evil deed,
Bill said this must be done at speed.

Kayleigh Byrne (10)
Aveley Primary School, Aveley

Head In The Clouds

I *zoomed* out of bed
I *swung* down the stairs
I *glared* at my breakfast
I *chomped* on my TV
I *slid* ready for school
I *dressed* in the car
I *staggered* ready to learn
But . . .
Found it hard as . . .
I'm all scrambled up since parents' evening's tonight!

Abbie Hession (11)
Aveley Primary School, Aveley

Oliver Twist Poem

Oliver walked through a jet-black gloom
when he entered the room that was to seal his doom.

He gazed at the hustle and bustle there
when a tall, treacherous man came walking, walking, walking
up the creepy stair.

The treacherous man was filled with fear
as Nancy gazed with her eyes full of tears.
He was wearing a cowboy's hat
and a coat that felt like a shaved cat.
Shoes like a brown fence with laces
and trousers that dangled as he took several paces.

Oliver was frightened of that treacherous man
but Bill used Nancy to help with his devious plan.
Nancy tried to take Oliver to keep him away from Bill
but Bill caught her and took her against her will.

Up the stairs Nancy was beaten badly
because Bill had hit her madly.
Bill tried to kill him but he got away.
Bill tried to run after him but he just had to stay.
In the end Bill was killed and Oliver hurriedly ran away.

Paige Ackroyd (10)
Aveley Primary School, Aveley

Eye-Catching Carp

Swimming and splashing
Darting and crashing
Eating and gurgling
Above the water shining and gleaming
Turning and thumping
Its silver and gold scales blinding people
And breaking the surface with a smash
Underneath he's wriggling and thrashing
Like a firing torpedo.

Rhys Frankland (10)
Aveley Primary School, Aveley

I'd Rather . . .

I'd rather eat fire,
I'd rather sleep on broken glass,
I'd rather call Mum and Dad a liar
Than lie on the itchy grass.

I'd rather take medicine,
I'd rather crawl to school,
I'd rather run 100 miles
Than not act really cool.

I'd rather poke my eyes out,
I'd rather be woken by lager louts,
I'd rather do most anything
Than eat my Brussels sprouts.

Amy-Louise Scott (8)
Aveley Primary School, Aveley

The Great Robins

Feeding and singing
Crying and eating
Scooping and gliding
Above a world dancing and loving
Hovering and thinking
Their red breasts glowing
And plunging down singing
Onto a world with life and death
Flapping and running
An elixir of joy and happiness.

Joshua Prayel (10)
Aveley Primary School, Aveley

The Horse

The horse in the field,
Galloping through the long grass,
Charging to the gate.

Waiting for its food,
Chomping away on the grass,
Eating hungrily.

Waiting two hours,
Until he can ride the horse,
On its back today.

Sarah McGoldrick (11)
Aveley Primary School, Aveley

My New Book

Can I read a book?
I love reading all day long
I want a new book.

Waiting to be read
It said I am pretty
I told it hello.

Can someone read me?
Everybody can read me
Hello everyone.

Billie Scott (11)
Aveley Primary School, Aveley

Oliver Twist

It was a cold and windy night.
A cat zoomed past and gave Oliver a fright.
He entered the dusty, old room
Which was about to seal his doom.

A man came up
The creaky stairs, the creaky stairs, the creaky stairs
And the room was full
Of hairs, of hairs, of hairs.

His name was Bill and beside him was Nancy
Although she was not rich her dress was fancy.
Oliver runs away to a different house
And at night it was as silent as a mouse.
Bill and Nancy kidnapped him
And their carriage looked kind of dim.

Nancy makes everyone sing a song
To distract Bill and Fagin but they don't get away
For long, for long, for long,
They don't get away for long.

Nancy was taken down
And when Bill fell into the river
He was about
To drown, to drown, to drown,
He was about to drown.

Sam Young (10)
Aveley Primary School, Aveley

Oliver Twist

Oliver wandered through the night of gloom,
When he entered the unpleasant room.
It was in the thieves' den when he met Nancy,
To evil Bill she had taken a fancy,
A fancy, a fancy,
To evil Bill she had taken a fancy.

Nancy is like a second mother to poor Oliver Twist,
She says when you meet wicked Bill you're taking a risk.
Bill is so mean he gets Oliver to do a shameful earner,
Oliver was caught, they said, 'You are a slow learner.'

Nancy will do anything for dangerous Bill,
Even when she knows it's Oliver he wants to kill.
Bill sent Nancy to kidnap Oliver,
She only did it because Bill's her lover.

Sweet Nancy started everyone singing on a song,
Bill looked round but where had they gone?
They were found under the bridge that night,
Bill killed Nancy, Oliver froze with fright,
With fright, with fright,
Bill killed Nancy whilst Oliver froze with fright.

On the bridge there was a shadow of a man's cape,
Oliver knew he could now escape.
Vicious Bill surrounded by a crowd,
Tried to jump but fell and drowned.

Samantha Drum (10)
Aveley Primary School, Aveley

Oliver Twist

Oliver entered a building that was full of dark and misty rooms.
He walked up the narrow staircase and unlocked a room of doom.
A tall, mysterious man with his wife by his side was waiting,
waiting, waiting.
A tall man was waiting for Oliver to arrive.

Oliver stood there in terror watching Bill and his wife
As Bill, the evil thief, pulled out a knife.
Nancy leaped across the room, putting herself at risk.
Jumping in front of Oliver, a chance that she could not miss.

Bill worried that he would spill the beans,
That left him shaking in his jeans.
Horrified at being locked up in a cell,
The story that he would not tell.
Bill plans to get Oliver back.
He kidnaps him and bundles him into a sack.

Bill was a dangerous and nasty man.
No one knew of his next plan.
Nancy threatened to tell the old bill
If he touched the boy or even kill.
Bill picked up a hammer and whacked her across the head
And hit her, hit her until she was dead.
Oliver's mouth was in his heart.
He wondered how Nancy could have played such a terrible part.

Bill threw his arms around his neck,
Running away over the deck.
He climbed up the ladder to the top.
Before he knew it he slipped and dropped,
Slipped and dropped
To his awaiting death, he slipped and dropped.

Rosie Munroe (11)
Aveley Primary School, Aveley

Oliver Twist!

Oliver arrived at a dark and mysterious room
which, inside, was going to be his doom.
He crept inside and who should be waiting there
but Nancy and Bill.
They were waiting, waiting, waiting,
Nancy and Bill were waiting for Oliver to appear.

Fagin, the thieving liar, was standing still in fear
while Nancy was watching, shedding a single pearl tear.
She leaped across the room and tackled Bill onto the dusty floor.
Nancy left Bill lying there reeling
and leapt towards Oliver with a motherly feeling.

Bill was an evil, hateful man.
Nancy did not know of his next plan.
Nancy told Bill she would tell the law
if he held the lad anymore.

Bill swiped a crowbar across Nancy's head,
he beat her and beat her until she was dead.
Oliver was shocked and shaking at what he'd just seen.
He was wishing it was all just a dream.

Bill grabbed the boy and ran away very fast
but Bill's luck was not going to last.
Police gave chase as they climbed up high,
Bill surely knew he was going to die.
As shots rang out he fell to the ground,
crowds gathered, not making a sound.
Bill lay dying, dying, dying,
Bill lay dying, dying on the ground.

Sophie Jeacock (11)
Aveley Primary School, Aveley

Oliver Twist

Oliver was shown around a building of pitch-black gloom.
Slowly he walked about the rundown building
when he came across a thieving room.

A tall, dark, mysterious man came creeping, creeping, creeping.
The tall, dark, mysterious man came creeping up the creaky stairs.
Oliver was shown around their den.
He marvelled at the golden, pearl treasure which was at least theirs.

Fagin, the thieving master, stared at him in fear
whilst Nancy in a corner shedding a single, watery, pearl-shaped tear.
Bill Sykes strode in the open, planning a thieving job,
nicking pots and pans off the gleaming cooking hobs.

Nancy, with her motherly love, motherly love, motherly love,
Nancy, with her motherly love, cared for Oliver like an injured dove.
Oliver, the ragged child, was taken away
whilst Bill Sykes was threatening he would pay.

Oliver was now living a happy life, was now not in fear
but Bill and Nancy were getting near, near, near,
whilst Bill and Nancy were getting near.

Where Bill and Oliver were, the top beam started to creak.
Bill slipped and fell into the murky dock,
to death he then meets.

Then the angry mob came running, running, running,
the angry mob came running through the crowded streets.

Oliver was now back with his cheerful family.
Now he can live very happily.

Allix Flowers (11)
Aveley Primary School, Aveley

Oliver Twist

Oliver ran through a dark, jet-black night of gloom,
when he entered the misty room
that was to seal his doom.

He gazed at the hustle and bustle there
then walking, walking, the treacherous man came walking
up the old, creaky stair.

He had a top hat on his head and black hair at his chin,
his soul was full of evil, he embraces sin.
His boots right up to his thigh,
his boots fitted with never a wrinkle,
he walked without a twinkle.
His stick without a twinkle,
his dog without a twinkle, under the jet-black sky.

A beautiful girl was sitting, sitting,
a beautiful girl was sitting on a green, mouldy chair.
Her face is full of fear which sadly she shares,
sadly shedding a well-loved tear
for her loved one close and near.

Nancy sang with all the adults so Oliver could run away
but Bill shot off to find them.
He did and killed Nancy, hit and killed Nancy to her death
where she lay, where she lay . . .

He grabbed Oliver and ran away to a lofty landing,
he passed a rope but he slipped and fell.
Oliver ran away with a lucky escape to live with the man
who wore a black cape.

Rebekah Brand (11)
Aveley Primary School, Aveley

Oliver Twist

Oliver walked into a night full of jet-black gloom
when he met a boy who offered him a room.

He put his things down and began to stare
when he saw a man come climbing, climbing, climbing,
a dangerous man came climbing up the rickety stair.

Another man walked up the stair,
he gave everyone a chill when he gave Oliver a glare.

He'd a black top hat on his head,
he looked as though he'd come back from the dead.

Nancy came into the room,
up the old, creaky stairs into the house of gloom.

She sang with all the men in her pub
which was like a magpies' den.

Bill throws Oliver on the ground,
he drags him away though Hell should bar the day.

They reach a forgotten river,
it gives Oliver a terrible shiver.

Bill finds them there,
he climbs the old stone stairs and hits Nancy to death.

Bill swings from a horrible tower,
at the bottom Oliver stays and he does cower.

Bill slips and falls to a horrible death,
so he has to draw one last deep breath
and that was the end of Bill
whose aim was to steal.

Elise Gurry (11)
Aveley Primary School, Aveley

Oliver Twist

Oliver limped weakly towards the bush which was fancy
whilst walking with a girl called Nancy
who had a rip upon her shoulder on her dress
and one nail painted differently than the rest.
Then they both saw Bill Sykes walking, walking,
they both saw Bill Sykes walking down the concrete road,
whilst talking.

But Nancy was in love with Bill
which didn't go so well but still . . .
Bill Sykes was a horrid man
and Nancy was as gentle as my gran.

Bill Sykes made Nancy join his plan
but Nancy would not follow.
He raised his hand and hit her cheek
but strongly she did not weep or swallow.

Bill Sykes told Nancy to kidnap Oliver
but Nancy would not go
so Bill Sykes told her she will be scared.
She tried to get out the door
but all was locked and barred.

So Nancy went to rescue Oliver
but Bill Sykes was following her.
Nancy was beaten to the bone
and she hit her head on a large, sharp stone.

Bill Sykes grabbed Oliver with a shiver
then he tried to cross the river
and then he found a rope
but the rope hit the ground
and evil Bill Sykes slowly drowned.

Danielle Bell (10)
Aveley Primary School, Aveley

Oliver Twist

Oliver walked through the dark, jet-black gloom,
unluckily he entered a room that was to seal his doom.
As he walked across the uneven floor,
a tall, enigmatic man came striding through the broken door,
striding, striding,
a tall, enigmatic man came striding through the door.

Oliver was told Bill Sykes was his name,
he tried in vain to be bold again.
Nancy helped Oliver over his fear,
later on, sadly, she shed a tear.

On his first job Oliver was caught,
considerate he was without being taught.
Surprised by Oliver was the rich man,
Nancy and Bill had a devious plan.

Nancy and Oliver made a getaway,
hoping to live another day
but Bill Sykes strikes.
He viciously ended Nancy's life,
life, life,
he viciously ended Nancy's life.

Bill Sykes' dog is called Bullseye,
he takes the police to where thieves lie.
Oliver and Bill attempt to escape,
Bill dies, Oliver is safe.

Nicholas Adams (11)
Aveley Primary School, Aveley

My Playful Kittens

My kittens are so playful
they never stop, they play all day
and never stop to sleep.
I wish they would calm down
but they never do.
They are cute, little, playful kittens.
They love to eat ham, Spam and cat food.
When I leave them I always miss them!
My kittens are so cute and cuddly.
They are mine forever
because they are my playful kittens!

Megan Webb (10)
Aveley Primary School, Aveley

Another Year Gone By

January begins the year
A new beginning is quite clear
February brings the dawns of frost
And valentines that have been lost
March brings the springtime
April brings the showers
May brings the blossom
June is blooming flowers
July sees the school year end
Long August holidays are a trend
September brings the harvest moon
October trees will be bare soon
November's fireworks light the sky
The speeding rockets fly up so high
December moon is so bright
Santa comes on Christmas night!

Tara Kelly (7)
Bearbrook Combined School, Aylesbury

My Unlucky Day

In the morning I got out of bed,
I went downstairs and my cat was dead.

I went in the bathroom to change my clothes,
I opened the mirror and broke my nose.

I went to my sister's because she was a nurse,
She was out so I nicked her purse.

With her money I went to the shops,
She caught me there so she called the cops.

The cops soon took me to the station,
They let me go but I was on probation.

I soon got through my big red door,
But as soon as I shut it I fell on the floor.

I soon thought home wasn't the place for me,
I stepped out the door and fell in some wee.

I soon got into my great old bed,
I won't be surprised if tomorrow I turn red.

Alannah Patrick-Robertson (10)
Bearbrook Combined School, Aylesbury

My Seasons Poem

Spring, spring, lovely spring
Children skip round a golden ring.

Beautiful summer is so great
And that's why people eat black apes.

Dull autumn, leaves fall down
Everyone's quiet and doesn't make a sound.

Winter, winter, snow and rain
Soon it will be spring again.

Yvette Agyekumhene (7)
Bearbrook Combined School, Aylesbury

World War

On a freezing cold night in Japan
England were getting attacked by Japan.
There was a very loud noise of bombs exploding.
The sparks crackled in the midnight air.
Thump of the rifle bullets going into bodies.
Hissing noises of the tanks moving in.
Whistling of the rocket launchers zooming through the air
With a tremendous flame lighting up the midnight sky.

Callum Giles (10)
Downing Primary School, Ipswich

Trees

Trees whisper in my ear
the smoothness of their bark is like the bumpiness of the sea.
The golden leaves rustling
and the colour changes to grassy green
then to golden sunshine.
Their roots crackling under the soil.
Trees are alive, don't cut them down!

Charlotte Priestley (10)
Downing Primary School, Ipswich

Storms

Rain splattering in the street
Thunder crackling in the clouds
Hailstones come rattling down
Going pitter-patter, pitter-patter
Getting harder and bigger, harder and bigger.

Amie Ruse (10)
Downing Primary School, Ipswich

Downing School

D owning is the best,
O uch, goes the pest.
W inning all the matches,
N o one misses the catches.
I gnore the paces,
N ot all the races,
G oing for the laces.

S ounding the whistle,
C atching the whistle.
H issing and missing,
O h, just listing.
O n a game,
L isten, there's no complain.

Daniel Suckling (11)
Downing Primary School, Ipswich

Dolphins

Splish splash
Splish splash
Dolphins in the sea.

Splish splash
Splish splash
Two jumped out of the sea.

Splish splash
Splish splash
The others looked at me.

Splish splash
Splish splash
They all swam out to sea.

Paula Emeny (10)
Downing Primary School, Ipswich

Trees

Swaying branches
In
The
Breeze
Chuckling through
The
Autumn
Leaves
Rustling
Whispering
Shimmering
Colourful
Sunlight
Shining through the glittering
Gaps.

Charmaine Forsythe (9)
Downing Primary School, Ipswich

That Car Goes Very Far

The car is blue,
The car is fast,
That car goes very far.

The car is red inside,
The car has a bed inside,
That car goes very far.

The boot is big,
The engine is wide,
That car goes very far.

The headlights are bright,
The oil is right,
That car goes very far.

Mathew Lambert (10)
Downing Primary School, Ipswich

Life-Giving Science

Potion bubbling chemicals,
Villagers think he's demonical.
Never meaning to be bad,
Always feeling kind of sad.
No one wants him, no one needs him,
He's a desperate, lonely soul.

Victor is his one true master,
Others believe he's a disaster.
The monster's only friend is a blind man,
Dracula wants him for his master plan,
To take over the world.

Wandering the world,
Looking for peace.
His ugliness he wants to hide,
He's even made a bride.

Together they live and love,
In their icy cove.

Joshua Osborne (11)
Downing Primary School, Ipswich

The Sea

Fish splashing,
Waves crashing,
Whilst the beach
Floor is crackling.

Aaron Cook (10)
Downing Primary School, Ipswich

Building Site

Loud, booming, swishing cement mixer,
Banging hammers,
Slopping of cement on the cracking bricks.

Aiden Josh Francis (10)
Downing Primary School, Ipswich

Sister Poem

S weet as syrup whenever it suits her,
Sour as old milk at all other times.
I s only good for messing things up,
Interfering where she's absolutely no business at all.
S he shows no brains, wit or humour but always simpers
Like a moron when there's something she needs.
T eases and torments you
Whenever you try to concentrate.
E xasperates all of your friends
With her excruciating charm and smarminess.
R educes everyone with sense to rage and frustration
And is ridiculously over-rated by everyone but *me!*

Rebecca Cantwell (11)
Downing Primary School, Ipswich

Books

Books chattering waiting to be opened
flattering their pages with our eyes
flapping page to page
they're all in competition with each other
vying for attention
they want us to hear their stories.

Charlotte Vince (10)
Downing Primary School, Ipswich

A Horrifying Limerick

I was teaching in the old schoolroom
When a werewolf charged in with a boom
So I squirted shampoo
And painted him blue
But he took me to his catacomb.

Emily Richmond (9)
Downing Primary School, Ipswich

Sun, Moon And Stars

The moon listens to our dreams
The night brings sweet dreams
The sun tells whispering stories
The dawn argues with the night
The sea kneads the stones
The moon teaches the sun how to dance
The sun tells night to go away
The evening hates the night
The stars show the sea their hearts.

Roberta Hunt (10)
Downing Primary School, Ipswich

Please Mr Teacher

(Based on 'Please Mrs Butler' by Allan Ahlberg)

Please Mr T,
This boy Tom Too
Keeps tickling my leg, Sir
What shall I do?

Go to the pier,
Run away from school,
Go and sit on the toilet,
Do what you think's best.

Please, Mr Honey,
This boy Peter Poly
Keeps hitting me, Sir
What shall I do?

Put your book in the bin,
Run to sea,
Run on to your home
And do what you think
But don't ask me!

Caroline Hall (9)
Great Linford Combined School, Milton Keynes

Please Mr Burdett

(Based on 'Please Mrs Butler' by Allan Ahlberg)

Please Mr Burdett,
This boy Tom Too
Keeps calling me nasty names, Mr,
What shall I do?

Go sit in the corner, munchkin,
Go sit in the sink.
Take your books on the playground, my love,
Do whatever you think.

Please Mr Burdett,
This girl Ellie Moo
Keeps punching me, Mr,
What shall I do?

Go sit in the kitchen, cupcake,
Go sit under the table.
Take your books to the dustbin, my petal,
Do what you are able.

Please Mr Burdett,
This girl Nancy Clue
Keeps scribbling in my books, sir,
What shall I do?

Go sit in the staffroom,
Go sit on Mr Pink.
Take your books to Mr Meehew,
Do whatever you think.

Please Mr Burdett,
This boy Naughty Loo
Keeps boffing in my face, Mr,
What shall I do?

Go sit in the corridor,
Go run away to the sea.
Take your books to the headmaster, my sweet,
But don't ask me.

Jennifer Watts & Abigail McKever (9)
Great Linford Combined School, Milton Keynes

Please Mrs Bernstein

(Based on 'Please Mrs Butler' by Allan Ahlberg)

Please Mrs Bernstein
This girl Sorry Sue
Keeps taking my glasses, Miss,
What shall I do?

Go sit on the shelf, dear,
Go sit in the sink,
Take your books outside, pumpkin,
Do what you think.

Please Mrs Bernstein
This girl Sorry Sue
Keeps pinching my leg, Miss,
What shall I do?

Go sit in the room, dear,
Go sit in the cupboard,
Run away to your house, my flower,
Help Miss Hubberd.

Please Mrs Bernstein
This girl Sorry Sue
Keeps taking my bear, Miss,
What shall I do?

Go sit in the toilet, princess,
Go sit on the stairs,
Run away to sea, my darling,
And find some cat hairs.

Tori Mallett (9)
Great Linford Combined School, Milton Keynes

Please Mrs Treverton

(Based on 'Please Mrs Butler' by Allan Ahlberg)

Please Mrs Treverton
This girl Clementine Clue
Keeps pushing me off my chair, Miss,
What shall I do?

Go and sit in the playground, love,
Go under the table,
Run away to sea, my dear,
Do whatever you're able.

Please Mrs Treverton,
This girl Clementine Clue
Keeps bossing me around, Miss,
What shall I do?

Go and sit on the roof, my dear,
Go and hide in your tray,
Flush your head down the toilet, my love,
Tell a person on duty at play.

Please Mrs Treverton,
This girl Clementine Clue
Keeps laughing at my work, Miss,
What shall I do?

Go and sit in the hall, my pumpkin,
Go and look at the sea,
Do whatever you can, my lamb,
Just don't ask me!

Lauren May Evans (9)
Great Linford Combined School, Milton Keynes

Please Mr Buler

(Based on 'Please Mrs Butler' by Allan Ahlberg)

Please Mr Buler,
This girl Verity Glue
Keeps reading my work, Sir,
What shall I do?

Go and sit in the loo, my love,
Go and sit in the swimming pool and sink,
Take your books in the playground, my dear,
Do whatever you think.

Please Mr Buler,
This girl Verity Glue
Keeps taking my ruler, Sir,
What shall I do?

Go and sit on the roof, my lamb,
Go sit under the table,
Take your books to the hall, my love,
Do what you are able.

Please Mr Buler,
This girl Verity Glue
Keeps taking my pencil, Sir,
What shall I do?

Keep it in your hand, honey,
Put it in your pants,
Keep it in your pencil case, my love,
Go and study the ants
But don't ask me!

Adam Pattle (9)
Great Linford Combined School, Milton Keynes

Please Mr Treverton

(Based on 'Please Mrs Butler' by Allan Ahlberg)

Please Mr Treverton,
This teacher Terry True
Keeps telling me off, Sir,
What shall I do?

Go sit in the office, dear,
Go sit in a van,
Take your pencil in the bushes, my buttercup,
Do whatever you can.

Please, Mr Treverton,
This boy Henry Goo
Keeps hitting me on the leg, Sir,
What shall I do?

Go sit in the bathroom, dear,
Go do your test,
Keep it in a cast, my pumpkin,
Do whatever you think's best.

Please, Mr Treverton,
This girl Clare Clue
Keeps hitting me on the head, Sir,
What shall I do?

Wear a crash helmet, dear,
Go run out to sea,
Go roll in the mud, my munchkin,
But don't ask me!

Rebecca Horton (9)
Great Linford Combined School, Milton Keynes

Please Mr Fowler

(Based on 'Please Mrs Butler' by Allan Ahlberg)

Please Mr Fowler,
This girl Henrietta Hue
Keeps pointing her witchy nails in me, Sir,
What shall I do?

Go and sit somewhere else, pookey,
Go and sit in the room that's pink,
Take yourself home, my munchkin,
Do whatever you think.

Please, Mr Fowler,
This boy Henry Drew
Keeps pinching my leg, Sir,
What shall I do?

Go and sit in the medical room, lovey,
Go and sit in a can,
Go and run round the playground, smartie,
Do whatever you can.

Please, Mr Fowler,
This monster Gangy Goo
Keeps scaring me out of my skin, Sir,
What shall I do?

Go take your dog for a walk, cooey,
Go and jump in the sea,
Go home and cuddle your mum, my baby,
But don't ask me!

Alice Murray (9)
Great Linford Combined School, Milton Keynes

My Dad

My dad is great
He's my best mate
He is so strong
Enjoys the odd sing-song.

Got a flashy car
He's my superstar
Men give dodgy looks
He's a superb cook.

Singers get jealous
So he does a cappellas!
Men want to be him
I get to see him.

I want to hug him
Cos I really, really love him.
Steve, that's my dad.

Gary Wilson (12)
Great Linford Combined School, Milton Keynes

Ode To Dictionary

Ode dictionary,
You're a non-ending brain provider,
You're a helpful piece of information,
Like a book that doesn't make sense.
Your words, your thin paper,
How you help me when I am in need of a spelling.
O thoughtful, helpful word processor.
How I will love you,
How I will worship you.
O dictionary.

Kirsty White (12)
Great Linford Combined School, Milton Keynes

Please Mr Treviton!

(Based on 'Please Mrs Butler' by Allan Alhberg)

Please Mr Treviton,
This girl Sour Soo
Keeps shouting in my face, Sir,
What shall I do?

Go and sit on a duck, dear,
Run away to sea,
Travel on a fly to Spain, my love,
Do whatever's to be.

Please, Mr Treviton,
This girl Mical Crew
Keeps spoiling my work, Sir,
What shall I do?

Hide in the cupboard, sweetie,
Shove her under the table,
Go and sit on the roof, my pet,
Do what you are able.

Sophie Dixon (9)
Great Linford Combined School, Milton Keynes

Wind

She travels through the air,
She is gliding all around us,
Her freshness is spreading,
Her delicate touch strikes through the trees,
She twists aggressively,
As we feel her relaxing breeze,
Her clumsy waves shimmer,
She's invisible, she is wind.

Sabra Abukalid (12)
Great Linford Combined School, Milton Keynes

Holes

Kissing Kate kissed
When she got bit she hissed
She kissed an onion picker
Boy, she did not bicker
She hated Trout Walker
Man, he was a talker
The sheriff wished he listened
Kate's lips glistened
When the school burned down
She left the old town
The onion picker's dead
'I'll be back,' she said
When she became an outlaw
She knocked on the sheriff's door
She shot him in the leg
And he began to beg
She stabbed him in the heart
His love for her fell apart
She ran to her dying place
She got called freckle face
She was bitten by a lizard
Her blood was cold as a blizzard
Here she did die
In her grave she does now lie.

Alexei Wallace (12)
Great Linford Combined School, Milton Keynes

Volcanic Journey

Visiting the peak of a vicious volcano,
Seeing the lava bubble and burn,
Seeing the rocks twist and turn,
Seeing boulders fall from the sky.

Seeing my hands shake with fear,
Seeing my feet tumble and fall,
Making it seem that I was never here at all.

Daisy Wooller (12)
Great Linford Combined School, Milton Keynes

Fruit Bowl

Fruit can be sweet.
Fruit can be sour.
But don't look at me
I am not sour.

Fruit can be juicy.
Fruit can be dry.
But don't look at me
I am not dry.

Fruit can be hard.
Fruit can be soft.
But don't look at me
I am not soft.

Fruit can be smooth.
Fruit can be rough.
But don't look at me
I am not rough.

So altogether
I am a sweet, juicy, hard, smooth fruit.
OK! What kind of fruit are you?

Tanya Ward (8)
Great Linford Combined School, Milton Keynes

Grass . . . In Winter

The grass, in winter, might as well not be there,
For nobody's allowed on it!
Dinner ladies say, 'Get off there!'
Mums say, 'It's too muddy!'
Dads say, 'We'll play another time!'
Teachers say, 'Not today!'
The grass might as well not be there . . . in winter.

Rose Ashbourn (12)
Great Linford Combined School, Milton Keynes

Food For Me

Mum with the tea cakes.
Dad with the chocolate.
Brother with the muffins.
Sister with the tea.
Dog with the steak.
Rabbit with the carrots.
Guinea pig with the sprouts.
Bird with the seeds.
And me, well, I have -
Teacakes,
Chocolate,
Muffins,
Tea,
Steak,
But not
Carrots,
Sprouts and
Seeds!

Ashley Rynsard (11)
Great Linford Combined School, Milton Keynes

The Sea

The sea can be stormy.
The sea can make fog.
The sea can howl
Like a naughty dog.

The sea can whisper.
The sea can wish.
The sea can dazzle
Like an angelfish.

The sea can dance.
The sea can sail.
The sea can swim
Like a beautiful whale.

Danielle Budd (9)
Great Linford Combined School, Milton Keynes

Magic, Magic

Magic, magic, mystical magic,
Wizards, witches, charms and spells.
Potions that will make you smell.
Flying broomsticks, magic balls.
A secret world much better than all,
Unicorns of silver, white, mystical creatures, manes of light.
Black cats, witches, wizards, frogs,
The gates of castles have winged hogs.
Werewolves, hippogriffs, skrewts and more,
Things that people don't adore.
All these creatures of magical kind,
But each of them have a spell to bind.
So many features hard to count,
And most of them are hard to mount.
Scarab beetles oozing puss can help to heal poison cuts,
Their wings are very thin and fine,
They live in tall and muscly pines.
Fairies, little balls of light,
That appear in happiness every night.
Goblins, gruesome, clever, evil things,
That hoard coins, goblets and rings.
Woodland creatures such as elves,
Naughty beings with a sense for gold.
Magic is a mysterious thing,
Like a bird of wisdom taking you under its wing.

Carys Miller (9)
Great Linford Combined School, Milton Keynes

My Dad

If my dad was a car, he would be a rusty old banger that would slowly
'putt-putt' along a cobbled road.

If my dad was a food, he would be a bowl of stale, mouldy porridge,
cheap and lumpy, sliding across the bowl thickly.

If my dad was a colour, he would be grey, dull and boring,
standing around all day doing nothing, getting nowhere.

If my dad was an animal, he would be woodlouse, small, pathetic
and ugly, crawling across a washbasin, slow and loosely.

If my dad was a plant, he would be a weed, useless and flimsy,
so weak, having to climb up a wall for support.

If my dad was a country, he would be Vatican city, a small country with
no population or popularity.

If my dad was an item of furniture, he would be an old,
good-for-nothing, well-used armchair, with bits coming off it
and patches littering its surface.

If my dad was a book, he would be an old, dusty, weather-beaten book
with pages falling out and torn pages at the back of the book.
He would be perched on the top of the bookcase, moth-eaten
and unread.

If my dad was a bird, he would be an owl, wise and intelligent
and he would realise that this is all a big, hilarious joke.

And would know that he is . . .
As fast as a Ferrari,
As tasty as lemon meringue pie,
As shiny as silver,
As sleek as a tiger,
As unique as a rare orchid,
As exciting as the USA,
As cosy as a duck-feather bed
And as intriguing as a James Bond thriller.

Oliver Giles (11)
Haddenham Community Junior School, Haddenham

Independent Bacon

Sorry, Sir,
We're out of bacon,
It took the bus
To Haddenham station.

Sorry, kids,
We've no more gravy,
It went to sea
To sink the navy.

Sorry, Ma'am,
We've no salami,
It marched right out
To join the army.

Sorry, chaps,
The spuds aren't here,
They had a touch
Of diarrhoea.

Sorry, Sir,
We're out of beef,
It's gone upstairs
To clean its teeth.

Sorry, mates,
We've no more trout,
They've not gone anywhere,
We've just run out!

Sam Shaw (11)
Haddenham Community Junior School, Haddenham

Night

She always comes out
Right after the days
On the small, small earth
Where she often lays.

Her face is so pale
Shining so bright
Sending out rays
Of silver moonlight

In her blue dress
That she mostly wears
For the silver sequins
She loves and cares.

She smiles down
On the little earth
While she whispers
For the night's birth.

Emily Saunders (10)
Haddenham Community Junior School, Haddenham

The Face Race

Tick-tock goes the clock, tick-tock.
There's a daily race on the clock face,
Three little hands in the face race.
Last is the hour hand, steady and cool,
Plodding along slowly, the short, fat fool.
Second is the minute hand, quick but not fast,
He isn't in first but he isn't in last.
In first is the second hand, unlike his name suggests,
Zipping past quickly, with no time for rests.
However fast these three might run,
No one's lost and no one's won.

Edward James (11)
Haddenham Community Junior School, Haddenham

The Dark Night Falls

The dark night falls
Like a huge, black sheet.

The window's closed
And the house locked up.

The birds settle down
And protect their young

And all is peaceful once more.

The foxes come out
To catch their prey.

The bats flutter about
Like hair in the wind.

The badgers crawl out
And slowly walk

And all is alive once more.

The cold wind howls
Through the bare trees.

The clouds move in
Like complex clockwork.

The moon is bright
Like a huge white bulb

And all is tense once more.

The wind gets stronger
And strains the trees.

The clouds give way
To the pouring rain.

The moon is hidden
Blotted out of sight

And all is starting once more.

The thunder hits the sky
The lightning forks out.

The rain crashing down
And dancing on the house.

The wind it whistles
Like a terrifying scream

And all is frightening once more.

The animals find their shelter
They quickly hide themselves.

The houses seem to struggle
To stay rooted to the ground.

The sea becomes restless
Like a cat in a cage

And all is fearful once more.

The dark night goes on
And seems to never stop.

The seconds drag on
Into everlasting hours.

The sun seems distant
Suspended far from here

And all seems weak once more.

The morning wakes up
Like curtains being drawn.

The people arise
And prepare for the day.

The birds start singing
Their sweet, cheery song

And the dark, old night has gone.

Stephanie Palmer (11)
Haddenham Community Junior School, Haddenham

The Battle Of The Cats And Dogs

The battle of the cats and dogs
Happened in late May
The howls and screeches deafened ears
In ways I cannot say.

Upon the lawn of Mrs Green
They stood in line to fight
Pulling out their bones or mice
As day faded to night.

The dogs were dressed from head to paw
In trusty canine gear
They showed their muscles to the cats
And gave the cats a sneer.

The cats were the calm and gentle kind
But hide a deadly whack
Like ladies of the snooty type
They flicked their hair right back.

The cats said, 'We will win this fight,'
With evil eyes of fear
The dogs replied, 'You'll be so scared
You'll never come back here.'

Like graceful ballerinas
The cats walked to their foes
The dogs with their karate skills
Just kicked them on the nose.

But then around the corner
Came Mrs Green afright
And from her gaping eyes she saw . . .
. . . creatures scattered in the night.

Charlotte Smith (11)
Haddenham Community Junior School, Haddenham

For My Parents!

For my parents
I'm the kind of kid
My parents don't want to be seen with
Because I'm the kind of kid who -

Talks too much
Sings in the shower
Says hello to lamp posts
Makes people laugh
Always laughing
Walks embarrassingly
Always telling bad jokes
Dances in the street
Sings in public
Talks to ducks.

Rebecca Everton (11)
Ladymede School, Little Kimble

For The Kids

I'm the kind of dad
My children don't want to be seen with
Because I'm the kind of dad who -

Dances on the street
Says hello to strangers
Nicks their sweets
Believes in tree land
Sings to the music in the shops
Does a load of voices
Sings out of the car window
Uses my kids as hangers
And
Kisses them at night.

Amy Bailey (11)
Ladymede School, Little Kimble

For Martha

I'm the kind of brother
Who my sister finds annoying,
She doesn't like to see me
For the rest of the day.

We have many fights
And I end up in pain.
She says that I started it
But I think she lies.

I'm the kind of brother
Who my sister hates to be with.
She always wants me out of her sight,
When she's playing a game.

Though sometimes she can be kind
And cares for me and cuddles me.
So I love my sister
And I hope she loves me too.

Martha Barnes (10)
Ladymede School, Little Kimble

For Theresa

I'm the kind of brother
My sisters don't want to be seen with
Because I'm the kind of brother who -

Helps my younger sister walk
Treats my younger sister like a baby
Shows off in front of my sister's friends
Calls my sisters 'Shrimp'
Always takes the front seat
Always posing in front of the mirror
Makes me happy when I'm sad.

Theresa Brooks (11)
Ladymede School, Little Kimble

For My Daughter, Francesca

For my daughter Francesca
I'm the kind of dad
My daughter doesn't want to be seen with
Because I'm the kind of dad who -

Tries to be serious but always cracks a smile
Waffles on for far too long
'This is the Hutt residence,' is what I say when I answer the phone
Dances to songs on Radio One
Nicks one of her sweets to see if they are poisonous
I talk to my friends in the supermarket
I sneakily take a fudge from the pick 'n' mix container
Sings out of tune
Tells cheesy jokes
But
I think I make her smile.

Francesca Hutt (11)
Ladymede School, Little Kimble

For My Sister

I'm the kind of brother who my sister
Doesn't want to be seen with
Because I'm the kind of brother who -

Tries to be a conductor
Embarrasses my sister on the phone
Tries to be funny when I'm not
Tries to play-fight my sister
Never lets her do anything
Dances in the street
Eats all my sister's food
Drives my sister nutty in town.
I get my sister into trouble
And
Lets my sister stay up late when I look after her!

Victoria Shipp (10)
Ladymede School, Little Kimble

For The Kids

I'm the kind of dad
My children don't want to be seen with
Because I'm the kind of dad who -

Sings on the street
Pretends to do the Rockin' Robin
Pretends to be a cheerleader
Shouts out funny names through the car window
Tests our food for poison
Dances in the car
Swerves on both sides of the road
Teases my mum about chocolate during Lent
Cackles like a witch
Gives them big hugs.

Elizabeth Brooks (11)
Ladymede School, Little Kimble

For Danielle

I'm the kind of dad
She doesn't want to be seen with
Because I'm the kind of dad who -

Sings wherever I go,
Does impressions of things my daughter's never heard of,
Helps strangers,
Puts gel in my hair and I'm 48,
Dances to music,
Puts the music on really loud in the car,
Tickles her,
And
Cuddles her at night.

Danielle Flynn Mushett (11)
Ladymede School, Little Kimble

For Emma

I'm the kind of brother
My sister doesn't want to be seen with
Because I'm the kind of brother who -

Goes to the toilet in the garden
Opens the front door in the nude
Answers the phone saying, 'Who's calling?'
Screams to get what I want
Eats like a fish
Drinks chocolate milkshake
Says, 'No I want my wellies!'
Sings The Grand Old Duke of York
Opens the fridge and says, 'Can I have something?'
And
Says, 'I love you three.'

Emma Simon (11)
Ladymede School, Little Kimble

For Chloe

I'm the kind of dad
My children don't want to be seen with
Because I'm the kind of dad who -

Sings in the shower
Nicks sweets
Loves to clean up
Poison tests food
Shouts, 'I love you' through the car window
Sings and dances in the kitchen
Stuffs balloons up his dressing gown
Pretends to be Frank Spencer
Tells the same doctor jokes every day
But
I make the children laugh.

Chloe Barr (11)
Ladymede School, Little Kimble

For Olivia

I'm the kind of mum
My children don't want to be seen with
Because I'm the kind of mum who -

Laughs loud on the phone
Sings out of tune songs in the bath
Calls Olivia embarrassing names really loud in *public*
Drives really slow
Gets hooted at on roundabouts
Wears really unfashionable clothes
Tells people off on the telephone
Dances in the theatre
But
Cooks really nice food.

Olivia Mansfield (11)
Ladymede School, Little Kimble

For My Kids

I'm the kind of dad
My children don't want to be seen with
Because I'm the kind of dad who -

Dances in the shops
Sings in the street
Eats all the food
Always cuts the grass
Always washes the car
Perfects the garden
Has a split personality
Shows off to his daughter's friends
Listens to his music way too loud
And lets his kids be free.

Hannah Thorpe (10)
Ladymede School, Little Kimble

Spooky Nights

S pooky things crawl at night
P eeling the fear off your skin
O ozing through you
O nly you are in the house
K icking footsteps on the floor
Y ou wouldn't dare to get down.

N oisy sounds under your bed
I nky shadows on the walls
G iving you a fright
H ouses are black with
T witching walls
S ucking up the light.

Liam Priestnall (8)
Lambourne CP School, Abridge

Something Singing

Tick-tock,
Went the bathroom clock,
Miaow went the cat,
Who wears a top hat,
Jack's playing football,
While Grace was at the mall,
I see a star,
Maybe I'm eating a Mars bar,
Ring, ring,
The church bell sings,
Silent is the world,
Wishing it could be,
One family.

Eloise Sladden (7)
Lambourne CP School, Abridge

My Best Friends

My best friends,
They stand by me whatever happens,
Funny, pretty, trustworthy,
As sweet as sugar,
As pretty as roses inside and out,
They make me feel good about myself and who I am,
They make me feel important, like I am on top of the world.
My best friends,
I am so glad that I have got them as my best friends
And I am so lucky.

Tayla McCloud (11)
Lambourne CP School, Abridge

Lunch Box

In my lunch box it is always bright.
I have Coke and Sprite.
I have a nice, hot, sticky bun.
I have lollies and lots of gum.
I have ham that is in a shape of a bear.
I have a fudge gingerbread man that stares.
That's what I've got in my lunch box today.
Oh, look at the time, it's lunchtime - hooray!

Georgia Anstiss (8)
Lambourne CP School, Abridge

Flowers

Flowers, flowers, flowers
Red, blue, yellow flowers
Mini, medium, jumbo flowers
Swaying, dancing, growing flowers
Blooming, smelling, fantastic flowers
Flowers, flowers, flowers.

Harrison Dunk (8)
Lambourne CP School, Abridge

Sharks

Sharks, sharks, sharks
Swimming round the ocean
Crunching up fish
Crunch, crunch, crunch
Speeding with its fin shining above the water
Swimming round sunken boats
Shining teeth glazing in the water
Sharks, sharks, sharks.

Jack Glass (8)
Lambourne CP School, Abridge

My Mum

She's as comfortable as a sofa.
She's as bright as a blue door, always open.
She's as beautiful as a flower.
As nice as a bumblebee.
As clever as a clock always telling the time.
As cute as a puppy, always cuddling me.
As happy as the sun.
Always smiling, like a clown.
I'm so happy she's my mum.

Rebecca Buckley (10)
Lambourne CP School, Abridge

Dolphins

Dolphins live in the sea,
Hopping and turning,
Hopping and turning,
Having lots of fun,
The wet water,
Splashing and
Splashing.

Hannah Marsh (8)
Lambourne CP School, Abridge

My Best Friends

My best friends
They are funny
Smart, silly, talkative
Like a parrot (one of them anyway)
Like a clown
I feel safe with them
Like a king surrounded by all the people in the world protecting me
My best friends
It reminds me how lucky I am to have friends like them.

Charles Miller (11)
Lambourne CP School, Abridge

My Pet

My pet rabbit, Snowflake's her name.
She runs about on the grass
And she goes really fast.
If my sister ever raced her
She would come last.
Snowflake scratches me and it hurts
But whatever she does I still like her.

Tanya Svilar (7)
Lambourne CP School, Abridge

Sharks

Sharks, they eat and eat fresh fish,
They swim and swim so they won't drown,
Their teeth are very, very shiny and sharp,
They live in salty, salty water,
They cannot jump because they're too fat.

George Pemberton (8)
Lambourne CP School, Abridge

Footballs

I saw a football the day I started school,
It was squashed flat, not like a ball at all.
I picked it up and put it in my bag
But when I got home I ended up quite sad.
Someone had taken my ball.
Yes, that was all
But it was mine.
My lovely football, quite divine.
I told my mum, she didn't care,
I didn't tell my dad, he'd swear.
I went to bed quite sad that night
And with my pillow had a fight.
I really, really was upset,
It really was hard to forget
But never mind, it's my birthday soon.
If I get a football I'll be over the moon.

Georgia Hutton (10)
Lambourne CP School, Abridge

My Dog Scooby

My dog Scooby,
A fully grown Great Dane.
Rough, tall, fast,
Like a giraffe reaching the tallest of trees,
Like a giant dinosaur.
It makes me feel like Mini Me.
He makes me feel happy.
My dog Scooby.
It reminds of me of Scooby-Doo, the movie.

Jordan Rampling (11)
Lambourne CP School, Abridge

The Hot Sun

The hot sun
Made millions of years ago.
Hot, big, strong,
Like a red ball of fire,
As big as four worlds.
It may make me feel small,
The hot sun
Keeps me alive.

Oliver Bickerstaff (11)
Lambourne CP School, Abridge

The Cheetah

The cheetah
Runs at sixty miles per hour.
Fast, agile, vicious,
As fast as the speed of light,
As vicious as a velociraptor.
It makes me feel slow,
As slow as a tortoise.
The cheetah,
It reminds me not to play cards with a cheater.

Luke Burrows (11)
Lambourne CP School, Abridge

The Great Sun

So bright and happy
Shiny, sparkly, all so bright
Like a golden patch
Like a big world of happiness
The sun is a golden wonder
I love the golden cloud
The great sun
It is a life binder that keeps us alive.

Sam Satchell (10)
Lambourne CP School, Abridge

My Dog Pepper

My dog Pepper
Is cuddly,
Small, funny, hyper,
Like a fluffy teddy,
Crazy like a madman.
He makes me very happy.
I feel like a giant towering over him.
My dog Pepper.
I feel so pleased to have such a great dog.

Jamie Seagrave (11)
Lambourne CP School, Abridge

The Speedy Cheetah

The speedy cheetah
Fastest land animal on the planet
Quick, elegant, athletic
Like a Ferrari when it rapidly moves to another place
Like a Ferrari
I feel that I am a cheetah
Like I am the cheetah, quick and athletic
The speedy cheetah
Reminds me how quick I am.

Joshua Allen (10)
Lambourne CP School, Abridge

Bugs

Blue bugs, blue bugs, sleeping in your shoe bugs.
Red bugs, dead bugs, crawling in your head bugs.
Black bugs, black bugs, they're on your back bugs.
Bugs are small and they crawl!
There are lots and lots of bugs and they're *everywhere!*

Ashley Hall (8)
Lambourne CP School, Abridge

My Brothers

My brothers
I have two
Funny, playable, lovely
Like little puppies
Like little kittens
I feel happy to have them
I feel happier than the happiest person alive
My brothers
Remind me how happy I am.

Mason Preston (10)
Lambourne CP School, Abridge

The Lion

The lion
One of the best hunters alive
Killer, sprinter, beast
Like a Ferrari car
It makes me feel inspired to run
It makes me feel ready to pounce
It makes me feel like the king of the jungle
The lion
A big beast on the loose.

Jake Rudd (10)
Lambourne CP School, Abridge

Fairies

Ditty, dancing, little dots,
Prancing round with glee,
Like to jump, dance and sing,
Spread their magic on everything,
Including me!

Fairies are great!

Bethany Corder (8)
Lambourne CP School, Abridge

Motorbike

The motorbike
The bike is red
Very fast, shining metal
Caps like silver
Like the sun in the sky
Red like a Ferrari!

It makes me feel cool
Like a bike in a café.
The motorbike.
It makes me feel I want one too.

Jack Gurrieri (11)
Lambourne CP School, Abridge

My Dog Jimmy

My dog Jimmy
Is very furry,
Tall, black, playful,
Like a baby kangaroo,
Lazy like a pig,
He makes me feel special,
Like everyone else is invisible.
My dog Jimmy,
He reminds me of an old man.

Charlotte Wilkinson (11)
Lambourne CP School, Abridge

Spring

Spring is colourful,
Spring is fine,
Because the flowers open up when it's time,
Pink, yellow, blue and red,
All dancing in the flower bed.

Grace Fitzsimmons (7)
Lambourne CP School, Abridge

I Love My Dog!

I love my dog, he loves a bone,
he loves it when I am coming home.

I love my dog, he loves a walk,
he listens to me when I talk.

I love my dog, he loves to chew,
he loves me when I am feeling blue.

I love my dog, he loves a brush,
he loves it when I am in a rush.

I love my dog, he loves a ball,
he comes running whenever I call.

He doesn't like it when I am away,
he wishes that I would always stay.

He loves it when I am home and safe,
I love my dog, he is my best mate!

Matilda McDonald Tait (10)
Lambourne CP School, Abridge

My Goat Amy

My goat Amy
She eats cheese and onion crisps
Happy, playful, clever
Like a miniature horse
Like a lonely girl who wants to play
I feel happy to be around her
Happy like a desert would be happy to have rain
My goat Amy
Reminds me what it would have been like to be alone.

Gemma Louise Stledger (11)
Lambourne CP School, Abridge

It's Spring All Around

It's spring all around.
In mid spring,
The bluebells ring,
The rabbits play,
The horses eat the hay.
It's spring in the fields.

In the sun
The children run,
It's like a dream
As they eat ice cream.
It's spring in the village.

Up the tree
There's lots to see,
Quite an amount,
It's hard to keep count.
It's spring in the forest.

Easter's back,
Buds start to crack,
Birds lay an egg,
Baby birds start to beg.
It's spring *all around.*

James Hunt (10)
Lambourne CP School, Abridge

Maths

I'm number crazy
I'm good at signs
2 quick for teacher
Work is on the *table*
Easy-peasy
Is my *label*
Maths is 4 me
Not a *fable.*

Rachel Moggridge (10)
Lambourne CP School, Abridge

The Head Teacher

He's a big rocking chair,
He's a loud, yellow door,
He's a funny hyena,
A seagull out in the open,
The smell of a hot, spicy curry,
The sound of rock music,
A lightning night with a crackling shower,
A bubbly drink,
A rock star!

Ellie Shillaker (9)
Lambourne CP School, Abridge

First Day At School

When I arrived at Crendon School
I really had no friends at all,
Lots of children there were cool
But no one on whom I could call.

On the first day in the playground
Walking round, a little shy,
Wondering if I'd ever find there,
Friends on whom I could rely.

In the classroom after break time,
Time was passing very slow,
Then a girl who seemed quite friendly,
Katy, came to say hello.

I came to Crendon in September,
Started school without a friend,
Now we are best friends forever,
Playing games without an end.

Jesse Kempner (8)
Long Crendon School, Long Crendon

School

It's 8.30, I'm on my way to school
Scootering, waving - calling hello
Run into the playground, meet my mates
Louis in top group and me below.

My uniform is tidy, it's assembly now
Teachers being fussy, kids in a row
Literacy and reading, getting ready for PE
Captains to be chosen, it might be me.

Eating my lunch as fast as I can
Trying to get out before Shirley sees
Run into the playground chasing my friends
Oh dear, someone's scraped their knees.

Mitch Gardiner (8)
Long Crendon School, Long Crendon

School Rap

I like playing in the swimming pool,
I think the swimming pool is very cool,
I like school at lunchtime,
Especially when the weather is fine.

I love Thursdays best of all
Because it's our turn to play football,
Running and playing on the pitch,
Be careful not to get a stitch.

PE is fun, as we soak up the sun,
When playing cricket I score a run,
When the ball hits the wicket it's not much fun,
So I just lay back and soak up more sun.

Shannon Govier (8)
Long Crendon School, Long Crendon

Wintertime

W inter is my favourite time of year,
I cicles are slippery and sharp.
N othing can be as warm as a mug of hot chocolate
by the crackling fire,
T obogganing in the silky snow.
E verybody hopes it's going to snow this year,
R esting by the fire is the best.
T he time of year we sing carols,
I 'm the best in my family making snowballs.
M y best thing about winter is . . .
E veryone has fun!

Isobel East (9)
Long Crendon School, Long Crendon

Winter Poem

W hite snow dripping from the sky like leaves from a magnificent tree.
I ce cracking like a falling branch.
N ew snow coming to cover the old, melting snow.
T rees swaying in the freezing fast wind.
E very day the days get colder and colder
Like a fridge that's been plugged in.
R aging wind freezes the lakes.

Nick Roberts (9)
Long Crendon School, Long Crendon

Winter

W ind hitting against my joyful eyes,
I ce covering flowers and bare trees,
N ight is as freezing as Antarctica,
T ucked up in my bed as hot as the sun,
E ating scrumptious hot pies,
R obins chirping in the morning and coming down to see me.

Jonathan Ian Airey (9)
Long Crendon School, Long Crendon

Bernwode Festival

B eautiful singing
E xcellent band
R inging ears
N o daydreaming
W onderful friends to be with
O rchestra playing tunes
D ads and mums come to watch
E veryone cheering happily.

F un pieces
E xciting, pushing conductors
S un-blinding lights
T errifying being on stage
I nteresting songs
V ery alert children
A id kit never used
L ong performance over, *phew!*

Eleanor Vickers (9)
Long Crendon School, Long Crendon

PE

I like PE, it is fun and exciting,
So all the games are very inviting
But changing clothes isn't so cool
Because you have to rush into the hall.

Now all my friends are good at balance,
They also say I have some talent,
Gymnastics is my worst within
Because I've never even visited the gym.

I love to jump and find it hard to stop
But best of all I love to hop,
RE is fun but PE is great
And it makes me lose my hate.

Kirsty Wells (7)
Long Crendon School, Long Crendon

The Clown Who Has Accidents

The clown who is very funny,
Was doing magic tricks
But they accidentally went wrong,
He ended up eating bricks.
He had some emergency help
In a hospital somewhere,
He walked around the hospital
And nearly lost his hair!

The clown is back doing his job now,
He's doing his magic tricks
But they accidentally went wrong,
He ended up eating sticks.
He had some emergency help
In a doctor's somewhere,
He walked around the doctors
And nearly lost his hair!

He's doing a different job now
Which is working in a circus,
He threw a big pie at the crowd
Instead it hit the workers.
The workers had emergency help
In their house somewhere,
They walked around the house
And actually lost their hair!

Laura Simons (9)
Long Crendon School, Long Crendon

Winter

W hining wind whistling through forests.
I n the house the windows frost with glistening light.
N either light nor dark in the midsummer morning.
T he wind is whistling through the trees.
E ar-splitting bangs as snow falls off the roof.
R obins singing the snow time song.

Leo Smith (9)
Long Crendon School, Long Crendon

A Riddle

My first is in cat but not in dog,
My second is in hot but not in cold,
My third is in stick but not in log,
My fourth is in flat and also in mould,
My fifth is in dead but not in alive,
My sixth is in grow and also in shrink,
My seventh is in jumped and also in dive,
My last is in blink and also in wink,
My whole is a living thing,
It would be impossible to keep the world going without them,
There are billions of these animals in the world.
What are they?

Louis Denis Stuart-Bourne (8)
Long Crendon School, Long Crendon

Sacred

S pecial books (like the Bible) are sacred,
A prized possession is sacred to us,
C hristians are sacred to God,
R amadan is sacred to Muslims,
E arth is sacred to everyone,
D ivision is sacred to teachers.

Ben Hambidge (9)
Long Crendon School, Long Crendon

Winter

W ind racing to my frozen hands,
I ce dotted around in my pond,
N ights cold in the shivering bed,
T rees covered with frost on mornings,
E very child is in the snow playing games,
R obins singing in the morning.

Lydia Kessell (9)
Long Crendon School, Long Crendon

My Neighbour

My neighbour who is creepy,
Likes stalking through the town
But you cannot see her dark face,
For she will knock you down.
But you know she's out there somewhere,
Waiting to catch her prey
But although she sounds terrible,
She would be kind if only you would play.

She senses your worst fears
And your terrified form,
As she leads your helpless mind
Into a volcano that is warm.
But you know that she is meddling,
For you can smell her awful smell
And although she cannot see you,
She can sense you very well.

Zoe McStay (9)
Long Crendon School, Long Crendon

Before The Doctors

Cooling Mum,
Calm me,
Sleeping magazines,
Hide me,
Terrifying nurse,
Hail me,
Resting people,
Let me go
To my safe, warm home
As the sun
Protects the lonely clouds
So may I
Escape the doctors
In this horrible building.

Lauren Hemmerdinger (9)
Long Crendon School, Long Crendon

The Treasure Seekers

We are the Treasure Seekers,
We search and hunt for gold,
Our adventures are very exciting
And many a story shall be told.

We travel to desert islands,
We've sailed the seven seas,
If people disobey us
We'll chop off their hands and knees.

We've discovered many crystals,
Ruby-red and sapphire-blue,
When we get the treasure on the deck
We share it out between the crew.

We're very fussy about what we drink,
It's rum or rum or rum . . .
There's Skully on the violin
And Crossbones on the drum.

We rescue maidens in distress
And hijack other ships,
We're also picky about what we eat
Prawns or fish and chips.

We are the Treasure Seekers,
We search and hunt for gold,
Our adventures are very exciting
And many a story shall be told.

This message that I send
Shows that it's the end.

Eddie Reynolds (10)
Long Crendon School, Long Crendon

My Gran

My gran is as silly as a clown.
Her hair is like the waves in the sea.
Her eyes are like flowers in amongst the grass.
Her face is like grass being blown by the wind.
She walks like her walking stick is a lead
And the dog on the end is pulling her
Like there's a food bowl on the end of the road with food in it.
When she sits down she is like a fish on dry land
Trying to get back to water.
When she laughs she is like a monkey tickling another monkey.
When she sleeps she is like a red kite hanging on a branch.
The best thing about my gran is
That when I press her nose
Sweets come out her sleeves.

Eleanor Stanley (8)
Long Crendon School, Long Crendon

School Rap

Well, here I am in the middle of the school,
Trying not to break the golden rule,
Now I'm not a teacher, I'm just a big boy,
And I'm not a bully and my name's not Troy,
While everyone is watching I shout out my name,
And as I do that, I feel the fame.

'My game is football,' I say to the school,
'My second best is diving in a pool
And when I'm mad I cool myself down
But now I'm wearing my dressing gown,
I can't get mad in my hottest coat
Because I'm eating a plate of porridge oat.'

George Hambidge (7)
Long Crendon School, Long Crendon

A Riddle

My first is in egg but not in chick,
My second is in cat but not in dog,
My third is in hog but not in pig,
My fourth is in octopus but not in squid,
My fifth is in long but not in tree,
My sixth is in Oxford but not in Aylesbury,
My seventh is in kick and also in punch,
My eighth is in animal and also in human,
My ninth is in tree but not in log,
My tenth is in igloo but not in house,
My eleventh is in ocean but not in land,
My last is in nut but not in shell.

My whole is essential for dolphins in the sea
It helps them find their food, you see!

Huw Thomas & Jacob Robinson (8)
Long Crendon School, Long Crendon

The Start Of A School Day

Come on, I'm not waiting anymore
Jump in quickly and shut the door
Have you got your homework book?
Quickly, then, have a look
We can't be late again today
What will Mrs Capitani say?
Have you got your sun hat?
Have you packed your cricket bat?
Did your teeth get brushed?
Now we are really rushed
At last we're on our way
But
Oh no! It's Saturday.

Oliver Picot (8)
Long Crendon School, Long Crendon

School

School, take a peek
At two of my favourite subjects:

Maths, maths
Easy-peasy
Ten times ten
Now let me think
Oh, now I see
It's . . . one hundred.

History, I love it
Digging in the past
Ancient Egypt
Gods and goddesses,
They believed in many of these,
Ra the sun god,
Floating over the sky,
Mummies lying in pyramids,
Waiting for their afterlife.

Francesca Edwards (7)
Long Crendon School, Long Crendon

School

I like school
It's rather cool
We go each day
To work and play
My favourite subject is History
Because it's full of mystery
We do lots of tasks
And sometimes wear masks
I like doing plays
Which often amaze
People in a different way
That's what I would like to do
Every day.

Emily Roberts (8)
Long Crendon School, Long Crendon

Aunty Dorothy

Today we lost a special aunty
She was kind and good
She always had nice biscuits handy
And tried the best she could.

Jamie and Toesy, her special dogs
Were loved by her a lot
They gave her joy
She gave them love
Our lovely aunty Dot.

We will miss our cosy chats
With cups of tea in hand
And miss her tasty cakes
The best in all the land.

Marcus Travers (8)
Long Crendon School, Long Crendon

Two School Riddles

Where would you find
Dinner ladies with no dinner,
Children, no teachers,
Sun and air,
No pens, no pencils,
But fun?

What is found in classrooms,
Labelled with names,
Found on classroom floors,
Also long and short,
Often in pain and sometimes -
Get chewed?

Cedric Louis Vennekens (8)
Long Crendon School, Long Crendon

A Riddle

My first is in in but not in out
My second is in done but not in start
My third is in terror but not in fear
My fourth is in iron but not in steel
My fifth is in float but not in sink
My sixth is in dungeon but not in prison.

My seventh is in you but not in me
My eighth is in cheap but not in expensive
My ninth is in tea but not in coffee
My tenth is in ice but not in water
My eleventh is in old but not in new
My twelfth is in now but not in later.

Katy Groves (8)
Long Crendon School, Long Crendon

A Riddle

My first is in move and not in stay,
My second is in ant but not in bug,
My third is in get and also in grab,
My fourth is in neat but not in messy,
My fifth is in 'in' but not in 'out',
My sixth is in farm and also in field.
My seventh is in animal but not in human,
My eighth is in clever but not in dumb,
My ninth is in egg and also in eggplant,
My tenth is in nine and also in nineteen,
My eleventh is in took and also in take,
You know what I am, I'm . . .

Chlöe Hykin (8)
Long Crendon School, Long Crendon

Reading

I like reading best
Poems and stories true
Tall tales all
And all the rest.

I like reading about cats and dogs,
Horses, ponies, all animals small
Spelling is harder, tables are tough
Reading is my favourite subject of all.

Natalie Karpa (8)
Long Crendon School, Long Crendon

My Riddle

My first is in scratch but not in nail
My second is in cat but not in dog
My third is in hammer but not in spanner
My fourth is in orange but not in banana
My fifth is in out and also in shout
My last is in Laurence and also in Elliott.
What am I?

Laurence Webb (8)
Long Crendon School, Long Crendon

My Winter Poem

W ind is beating against my frozen face.
I cicles keep on dropping on my freezing cheeks,
N ight winds are pushing me back through the freezing wind,
T he twinkling stars are frozen in the frozen sky,
E veryone is in a warm coat or something,
R obins singing wonderfully in the morning.

Callum Watson (9)
Long Crendon School, Long Crendon

My Poem That I'll Never Forget

I like playing with my friends,
I hope the fun will never end,
I like playing lots of games,
The ones I play are never the same.
I like doing lots of art,
Somehow it makes me feel smart.
I like making lots of cakes
And decorate them with sprinkles and shakes.
I like playing with messy things,
Like clay, papier mâché and other stuff as well
But I've forgotten one more thing . . .
Oh yeah! It's PE.

Emily Davis (8)
Long Crendon School, Long Crendon

The Moods Of The Sea

Tranquillity roams the seabeds,
Serenity rules the waves.
The sand is made of shimmering gold,
Seashells glisten in the sunlight.
Treasures are found by the sea.

A storm has struck,
The ferocious waves hurtle against the jagged rocks.
My heart pounds faster than before,
As my wonderful world disappears.

Eleanor Tiplady (10)
Long Crendon School, Long Crendon

Summer Poem

Wake up,
Summer's here,
Summer breeze,
Fully grown trees,

Mown lawn,
Buzzing bees,
Children laugh,
Playing outside,
Balls to kick and bikes to ride.

Summer's here,
But winter is near!

Nicola Sara Evans (9)
Long Crendon School, Long Crendon

Gran

My gran is as soft as a lily
Her eyes twinkle like stars
She stands up like a flower
And has ultimate powers
She makes me laugh 'til I drop
She is my
Gran!

Lauren E Rook (9)
Long Crendon School, Long Crendon

Scuba - My Best Thing

Scuba
Is my best thing
And when I do it, I
Enjoy my lesson with my friends
Each time.

Kian Guerzoni (9)
Monks Risborough CE Primary School, Princes Risborough

The Caretaker

I walked into the class one day
And saw our caretaker Mrs Gray
Rummaging through the teacher's drawer
And throwing everything on the floor!
It was so strange!

I asked her, 'What *are* you doing?'
I was surprised when she started coo-cooing!
She ran round the classroom like a bird,
I thought to myself, *this is absurd!*
I wondered what she'd do next!

She climbed on our desks and on the teacher's chair,
Everyone began to point and stare.
This made her angry, like the Hulk,
She roared at the children and made them sulk.
Then it went quiet!

We heard a shrill voice,
'Get down from there now, you have no choice!'
Mrs Gray climbed down from the ceiling.
The next thing we saw wasn't very appealing!
That was the most weird day ever!

Kirsty Abbott (10)
Monks Risborough CE Primary School, Princes Risborough

The Beach

I can hear the waves as they hit the shore as the white foam runs away
As the sound drifts away into the still night air
Then it comes again and echoes, the last breaking the silence
The stones as clear as ever in the beautifully moonlit shore
And becomes a black lake as calm as ever
I still stayed to watch the beautiful scene riding way into the distance.

Stephanie Grigg (10)
Monks Risborough CE Primary School, Princes Risborough

My Sister

My sister is friendly
My sister is loving
My sister gives me sweets
My sister helps me when I am hurt.

I love my big sister
When I am bored she plays with me
When my dad shouts at me
She sticks up for me.

My sister lets me go on the computer with her
Me and my sister love each other
Even when we fight
My sister is the
Best!

Stephen Griffiths (10)
Monks Risborough CE Primary School, Princes Risborough

My Dog Trigger

My dog Trigger is the best,
He likes to have a lot of rest,
Trigger is very playful,
But he is not careful.

Even though he has a shot,
He is greater then the lot,
He always wants to run around,
Also he likes to dig in the ground.

I take him up the woods,
When Trigger isn't naughty I give him some goods,
But when he wants to go swimming,
When we take him he is shivering.

Matt Pursell-Danks (10)
Monks Risborough CE Primary School, Princes Risborough

My Pets

Cats pouncing and jumping,
Fluffy and playful,
Different colours - tabby and grey,
So beautiful.

Fish in the fishbowl,
Relaxing and having fun,
Colourful in gold and silver,
Basking in the sun.

Horses in the field,
Frolicking and playing games,
Grazing while the sun goes down,
Riding in the country lanes.

Chickens in the shed,
Only two chilling out,
They haven't got names,
Clucking up and down, pecking about.

Amy Smith (10)
Monks Risborough CE Primary School, Princes Risborough

My Hamster

My hamster was called Sparks
She had orange fur
She would eat fruit, hamster food and toast
She drank lots of water from a bottle
She made her bed from sawdust and fluff
She slept in the daytime
She played in her cage
We put Sparks in her ball and she rolled around
We were happy watching her play
But when she died we were very sad.

Laurence Catterall (10)
Monks Risborough CE Primary School, Princes Risborough

Fireworks

Curling, curling in the sky
Reaching, reaching into space!
So sorry to see them go, bye-bye
So high they may reach another race.

Look, there goes a big one
The *bang* so deafening in my ear.
Fireworks confused not to see the sun
People set them off with no fear!

These fireworks are shapes of flowers
Lots of them looked like they had powers
Millions coming up in a storm
Colours so bright they make me feel warm.

Michael Le Quesne (10)
Monks Risborough CE Primary School, Princes Risborough

My Cat Oscar

M y cat Oscar's fat and old,
Y ears and years he's been brave and bold.

C atching mice was his favourite thing,
A lways climbing up the trees
T he birds now just laugh and sing.

O ur cat Oscar is awfully lazy,
S itting inside waiting to be fed.
C atching mice is too athletic for him
A ll he does is sleep in the sun,
R ight now he's most likely to be sitting inside watching TV.

James Hinton (10)
Monks Risborough CE Primary School, Princes Risborough

My Friend

My friend is a good friend
She is always right
The proof she is a good friend
We never have a fight!

My friend you will never be able to see
As she lives away from me
She doesn't come round very often
As she is invisible.

I don't really care
That everybody stares
When I talk to her
I promise she is really there.

Reanne White (10)
Monks Risborough CE Primary School, Princes Risborough

Summer

Hot and scorching in the sun
always playing around
having water fights and going to the park
that's what we call *fun!*

Having ice lollies to cool you down
always going swimming
having friends round to come and play.

We've finished summer
the time is passing on
we're back to summer again!

Sophie Morris (10)
Monks Risborough CE Primary School, Princes Risborough

My Cat Baggy

I have a black cat,
Who snuggles up on our mat.
When he was born he was small,
And now his tail stands up tall.

When dinner's there he goes slurp, slurp,
He chases birds that go twerp, twerp.
He likes food and will always eat,
He mainly likes the finest meat.

I have a cat called Baggy,
When he walks his tail goes saggy.
I love my little kitty cat,
Nobody can change it and that's that!

George Stone (10)
Monks Risborough CE Primary School, Princes Risborough

My Pet Guinea Pig

My pet guinea pig is very playful.
My guinea pig is very colourful.
My guinea pig is so scared of loud noises.

He eats guinea pig food with celery.
He falls asleep when I come home from school.
After twenty minutes he is awake.

I put him on the grass in the grass hutch.
I really, really like my guinea pig!

Rhys Brown (10)
Monks Risborough CE Primary School, Princes Risborough

My Friend Chris

Me and my friend Chris skate together,
We are great friends, we have not fallen out,
He makes me laugh at funny jokes,
I think we will be mates forever.

He taught me skateboarding tricks I didn't know,
He's the best friend I could ever have,
He lives in the house next to me,
I wish he was my brother because he is a great friend.

Kiren Barlow (10)
Monks Risborough CE Primary School, Princes Risborough

My Rabbit

My rabbit is always fun
The way he jumps in the sun.
He nibbles a carrot from one end
When he's finished he hops again.

At the end of the day he decides to stop
He jumps into his hutch and then *flop!*
He falls to sleep without a sound
Even in his dreams he hops around.

Ryan Stritch (9)
Monks Risborough CE Primary School, Princes Risborough

My Cat Sweepy

He chases birds and mice,
He thinks they taste so nice,
He has a thing for breaking toys,
Especially my brother's army boys,
He has a sweet tooth for fish,
He gives me a cheeky grin
That asks for a fish.

Heather Cross (9)
Monks Risborough CE Primary School, Princes Risborough

My Brother

Big and tough,
and always rough,
teases all the time.

Maybe sometimes lazy,
mostly always cool,
always good at everything.

He'll get me in a stress,
or I will make him moody,
just so big and strong.

He sometimes comes out to play,
that's only on my lucky day,
he just stays locked up in his room.

Even on a sunny day,
he has friends who will come over,
that's when I don't want to be around.

He can be very funny,
always jokes around,
my brother is the best!

Joe Jones (10)
Monks Risborough CE Primary School, Princes Risborough

My Pet Biscuit

If she sits and paws she gets a treat.
She can open the fridge and eat all the meat.
She barks at everyone that goes by.
She chases cats quicker than I.
My dog Biscuit is fat and lazy.
But she's a dog and I love her.

Jack Rice (10)
Monks Risborough CE Primary School, Princes Risborough

My Killer Cat!

My cat is very weird,
Because of his very small brain
He thinks he's an army man outside
But inside he's proud and vain.

Most of the time outside,
He's like a troop in a battle
But, of course, inside,
He is like he's on a horse on a saddle.

At night, inside,
He cuddles up with you
But much later on,
He kills birds too.

So my cat
(You could call him a killer cat)
Outside he kills,
Mice and rats.

Leah Kelly (10)
Monks Risborough CE Primary School, Princes Risborough

Animals' Actions

Bunnies bouncing,
Cats pouncing,
Snails going,
Owls knowing,
Dogs barking,
Fish larking,
Tigers scratching,
Birds hatching,
Blue tits singing,
Big cats bringing
Food home.

Rebecca Vieira (10)
Monks Risborough CE Primary School, Princes Risborough

My Cool Cat Bella

My cool cat's name is Bella,
She loves to go shopping,
She buys rings, earrings and jewellery,
In Bella's spare time before a party,
She makes herself all sparkly and gleam,
The prettiest cat in the town.
Bella is my cool cat!

Pollyanna Saunders (10)
Monks Risborough CE Primary School, Princes Risborough

My Dog

My dog has a tail that waggles all day.
He sits around playing all the time.
It's 7.00am so he goes and gets his lead ready for his walk.
When he comes back home from his walk
He has a great big yawn and falls asleep.

Sophie Giles (10)
Monks Risborough CE Primary School, Princes Risborough

T-Rex - Cinquain

T-rex
on its tall legs
walking through the forest
killing his prey and eating it
run now.

Thomas Robertson (9)
Monks Risborough CE Primary School, Princes Risborough

Woolworths

In Woolworths it smells
of sweets.

Sitting there waiting to be bought
are boots that are even denim.

And to one side there is stationery,
like fluffy pens and pencils
swaying
in the refreshing breeze.

The lights around are dim.

The clothes seem to bring people
especially girls
and pull them in!
And they make their mums buy something!

And the sounds in the background
make you want to shout,

'I love this place!'

Stacey Green (10)
Murrayfield CP School, Ipswich

Where Is It?

Where's the pair of shoes
I was wearing round the park
When I was four?
Worn out!

Where's the blanket
I chewed on
When I was three?
In the wash!

Jazmine Lambert (7)
Murrayfield CP School, Ipswich

I Love You!

I love you
Shops,
Even though
You don't give me anything
For free.

I love you
Mum,
Even though
You don't let me go to my
Friend's house.

I love you
Swimming pool,
Even though
You don't have a slide.

Lauren Watchman (8)
Murrayfield CP School, Ipswich

I Love You . . .

I love you, street.
Even though
the boys ride their bikes!

I love you, school.
Even though
you smell like hot dinner!

I love you, park.
Even though
you don't have much apparatus!

I love you, school.
Even though
we have to put up our hands!

Brandon Stannard (7)
Murrayfield CP School, Ipswich

Deep Questions

How many people are there with my name?
How many stars are there?
Are there any other planets with living creatures on?
Who invented space?
Will I ever tell the future or the past?

Will I ever be a pop star?
How many nerves are there in my body?
Who invented the names of shops?
Will the world ever end?
Will I ever tell the future or the past?

How many friends will I have when I'm an adult?
Will I ever be a celebrity?
How many shops in Ipswich?
Will everyone be able to walk one day?
Will I ever tell the future or the past?

Katie Goodwin (9)
Murrayfield CP School, Ipswich

I Love You

I love you, school -
even though
the pens run out!

I love you, shops -
even though
you don't have toys.

I love you, school -
even though
you make me do work!

I love school!

Katie Prentice (8)
Murrayfield CP School, Ipswich

Do People Tell The Truth?

How old will I be when I have children?
What killed dinosaurs?
Can life ever be the same as before?
How long has the Earth been here?
Will I ever know if people are lying or telling the truth?

When were cavemen on Earth?
How long were dinosaurs on the Earth?
Why was Earth invented?
When will my life end?
Will I ever know if people are lying or telling the truth?

How much water is there on the Earth?
Will God ever die?
Will I ever have another brother or sister?
What will happen to me when I die?
Will I ever know if people are lying or telling the truth?

Hannah Yule (9)
Murrayfield CP School, Ipswich

A Philosophic Poem

Who was the first human on Earth?
When did the world begin?
How did things change?

How many computer companies are there?
What language did ancient Egyptians speak?
How did things change?

How does the world end?
How many stars in the sky?
How did things change?

How many hairs on my head?
What language did the ancient Greeks speak?
How did things change?

Callum Kerr (9)
Murrayfield CP School, Ipswich

The Hobbit

The one ring to rule them all
The one hobbit to hold it
Travelling to save the world
We are disturbed
Out comes Gollum
Tricking the hobbit
One by one we die
Fighting the Uruk-hai
Coming from the Shire
We finished the journey
To save the world
We are smaller than men
We all live in Middle Earth
We have little hairs on our backs
We love to eat
We are very slow
We need your help
War is not a place for a hobbit.

Bethany Theodore (8)
Pirton Hill Junior School, Luton

Wrestling

Out from the entrance
and into the ring
slams, hits and bans
and a roar from the fans
I won, ding, ding, ding
Now out comes King
and a punch and a kick
Ow! That was quick
then off King goes
while I'm in a doze.

Shaan Sagoo (11)
Pirton Hill Junior School, Luton

Fairy Tales

Once upon a time a fairy tale written,
Puss in Boots once born was a kitten.
Cinderella, the fairest of them all,
More beautiful at the prince's ball.
Sleeping Beauty received a kiss,
Because the prince couldn't resist.
Snow White was very clean,
She was always nice but never mean.
Peter Pan, Peter Pan,
Beat the pirates if you can.
Pinocchio never learns,
Pinocchio don't tell lies or else your nose will grow.
I've come to the end of my poem,
Thanks for listening and your good doing!

Kieran Todd (11)
Pirton Hill Junior School, Luton

My Family

My nan is as funny as a seal,
My grandad is as old and as wrinkly as a bulldog.
They are both as happy as can be.
My dad is the funniest of all.
Posh mum is perfect like a poodle dog.
Dad is a monkey, like I said, he's the funniest.
Sam is as boring as a sheep
And is the youngest of all.
He is as mad as a parrot doing roly-polys.
All my family are the best
And the most special of all.

Sophie Draper (10)
Pirton Hill Junior School, Luton

Football

F ootball is my hobby.
O bviously I am good.
O n pitch I'm the best.
T o score is simple for me.
B all control is hard but I will manage.
A ll the time I play the whole game.
L ots of the time, the whole tournament.
L iverpool is my supporting team.

Samuel White (10)
Pirton Hill Junior School, Luton

Off To The Seaside

Playing in the sea,
building sandcastles for me.
Oh no, it's getting hot,
how about an ice cream?
I'm back inside the pool,
feeling nice and cool.
Come on it's time to go,
bye-bye, beach, I have to leave.

Jasmine Williams (9)
Pirton Hill Junior School, Luton

Fire!

O mighty fire, O mighty fire,
Please don't burn me, I'm not a liar.
With your bright red flame,
If you burn me it will be such a shame.
Fire, fire, why do you hate water?
I put you out, I'll be done for slaughter.

Alasdair White (11)
Pirton Hill Junior School, Luton

My Sister

M is for mad as a monkey.
Y is for yelping when we play.

S is for my sister, happy she could be.
I is for intelligent, good at her work.
S is for sisters, good ones we are.
T is for teenager, that's what she is.
E is for exciting as can be.
R is for roast dinner which she does not eat.

Hayley Russell (11)
Pirton Hill Junior School, Luton

The Burglar

Goldilocks breaks in, burglar!
While the three bears walked out
Waiting for the porridge to cool.
No porridge for baby bear,
Goldilocks stole it,
After criminal damage to his chair.
All too tiring for Goldilocks,
Asleep on poor baby bear's bed.
No wonder they were so mad!
Wouldn't you be?
So why are they portrayed as bad?

Alistair Smith (7)
Pirton Hill Junior School, Luton

Summer

The sun beams down like a turned-on light bulb.
The grass is fresh celery.
The trees are umbrellas hanging over you for shade.

Kieran Madden (10)
Pirton Hill Junior School, Luton

Dogs

The boy was walking fast
The dog's teeth
Were as sharp as when you see
A knife
Slicing through meat.
The boy slowed down.
The dog's tail
Started wagging
Like a fan
On a hot, summer's day.

Andre Collins (11)
Pirton Hill Junior School, Luton

Swimming

Bouncing,
Pouncing,
Sliding, diving,
Dunking,
Quickly racing,
Gliding, sliding
Swimming
Finishing
And winning.

Amy Graham (9)
Pirton Hill Junior School, Luton

I Like Swimming

I like swimming in the pool
The light blue water keeps me cool
I was very happy in the sun
It was lots and lots of fun.

Louise Gibson (8)
Pirton Hill Junior School, Luton

My Friends

My friends are really special
they care for me day by day.
They're really, really kind to me
and they shine in a special way.

my friends, we may lose contact
but that still doesn't bring me away
from the memories happy and special,
the thoughts are here to stay.

My friends are not just special
they're more than I can say,
we will be friends forever,
no matter what happens each day!

Jemma Morrin (11)
Pirton Hill Junior School, Luton

The Wind

The wind is pearly white,
And also very bright.
It whistles around
And makes quite a sound
That keeps you up all night.
She may be cold
Or maybe even bold,
Nobody will ever know.
The wind has a friend called Snow,
Who goes down very low.
Weather works in such wonders
Because the next thing you know it thunders!

Rebecca Kent (10)
Pirton Hill Junior School, Luton

My Imaginary World

When I was a girl, just like yourself,
I always got bored.
So I just thought and thought for a while,
My eyes lit up, I knew my brain was thinking.
I know what to do, let's go to the jungle!

Pushing my way through the great, green bushes,
Roar! Is that a lion I can see in the distance?
Oh yes, it is, run!
Think! Think! Think!

I'm getting swept away to the Arabian deserts,
The silky sand is blowing in my face.
A great figure is lifting up, a great pyramid I can see.
I'm really scared!
Think! Think! Think!

I wonder where I am? It looks a lot like a messy room.
'Hey, what are you doing? Get back to bed.'

So here I am, an old lady, just sitting here all day.
The only thing that amuses me is my imagination.
Let it run wild!

Adelaide Hetherington (11)
Pirton Hill Junior School, Luton

The Tiger

He prowls in the long grass waiting to hunt down his food.
His big feet go stamp, stamp on the dry, cracked floor.
His lovely orange fur glistens in the sun.
He hunts for a shaded place, so hot he feels he's on fire.
Nowhere shaded as he gets hotter and hotter.
What's this he sees? It's shade.
He walks proudly to the shade and lays and rests
Ready for a new, hotter day.

Alicia Burton (11)
Pirton Hill Junior School, Luton

Three Little Pigs

Three pigs were playing with their friends
'Watch out for wolf,' their mother said
But as you will see
It was not he
Who caused their woe
A tennis racquet on the head
The first of the three pigs was dead
A red house brick
Pig was not quick
The last of them went running in
'My brothers' heads are quite stoved in.'
His mother turned, began to frown
The whole house shook and fell down.

Jordan Simpson (8)
Pirton Hill Junior School, Luton

Goldilocks

Greedy Goldilocks
Out in the woods
Laughing her way through the bears' house
Damaging baby bear's chair
I loved the little chair
It looked so comfortable!
Overeating hot porridge.
Climbing
Kick her way upstairs.
Sleep in a bed that is not hers!

Natalie McFarlane-Rowe (8)
Pirton Hill Junior School, Luton

What Could It Be?

When I was little
I wouldn't go to sleep
All I could hear
Bump, bump, bump!
All through the day
All through the night
All I would do is pray
Because of all the frights.

After a while
I got really tired
Because of the
Thump, thump thump!
I would shiver
With all my might
Then with a slight quiver
I heard a bump in the night.

Chelsea Mason (10)
Pirton Hill Junior School, Luton

Sport

Football's good,
Rugby's better,
Water polo is so much wetter,
Netball is just so boring,
You could even end up snoring,
Volleyball is quite fun,
Jumping about in the sun.

You must have seen the Rugby World Cup,
A drop kick from the fly-half up
Until it went through the posts 20-17
17-17 it could have been.

Michael Ward
Pirton Hill Junior School, Luton

Timmy's Day Off School

Timmy woke up early one day,
He said, 'Are we going to school today?'
'No because it is Saturday.'

Timmy's mum was in the kitchen,
Washing up the dishes.
Timmy was in the other room,
Making exciting wishes.

His friend Ben was at the door,
While Timmy was cleaning the kitchen floor.
He said to Ben, 'Do you want to see my den?'
'Alright,' he said, 'but I've just got out of my cosy bed.'

When he got there he had a big surprise,
His den was full of nasty flies.
'I'd rather go home and rest in bed,
I will rest my head instead.'

Nathan Kirwan (11)
Pirton Hill Junior School, Luton

Goldilocks

Goldilocks eats the bears' porridge
Oh no! What a pity
Look, she's broken a chair!
Dozing in bed
In come the bears
Look! Who's that there?
Out! Out of here!
Catch her! Catch her!
Kick her out of here!
Stick her in goal!

Jordan Crownshaw (7)
Pirton Hill Junior School, Luton

Goldilocks

Grrr! Keep out of our house!
Other people's property
Lock her out!
Drama queen! Singing at the top of her voice
Into everything!
Lock her out!
Other people's property,
Cheeky girl!
Kicking up a fuss
Stealing the bears' food!

Charlotte Cochrane (8)
Pirton Hill Junior School, Luton

SATs

SATs are really boring
They make me ill in the morning
I don't really understand
They should be completely banned
In the test
Just do your best
That's all you can do
I'll just give you a clue
You do them on the 10th of May
Don't worry about them, just relax.

Kirsty Bradbery (10)
Pirton Hill Junior School, Luton

Pokémon

Pokémon may just be a game
But they sure do have some radical names.
They can fight, they can fly
But they never ever die.

Stephen-Kamrin Boyd (10)
Pirton Hill Junior School, Luton

My Pets

I have a dog,
She's as long as a log.
She chases cats
And sits on mats.

She doesn't like being left alone
But she loves her great big bone.
She's bigger than a bee,
She's smaller than a tree.

I also have a cat
Who chases rats
And sits on mats.
She's bigger than a mouse,
She's smaller than a house.
She likes climbing trees
And she likes catching bees.

Kate Atcherley (9)
Pirton Hill Junior School, Luton

Olympic Games

Every 4 years, you'll hear people cheer
For the Olympic Games.
I think they're great 'cause we stay up late,
Watching the Olympic Games.
Now we're in 2004, the Olympics will begin.
I hope this year's much better
Because it will be much more entertaining.
If I was to make up my own sport
I would be so glad
Because I'm a sporting person,
I would tell it across the land.

Shane Sutton (10)
Pirton Hill Junior School, Luton

Eid

Eid is a celebration for Muslims,
Eid is a time of happiness,
Eid is when you go to your cousin's,
Eid is when people have decorations,
Eid is when you get money,
Eid is a very joyful time for Muslims,
Eid is when you wear your new clothes and shoes,
Eid is when you go to the mosque,
Eid is when you go out,
Eid is where you eat chapatti,
Eid is where you eat,
After mosque we Muslim brothers greet each other,
At the end of the day there is another year for Eid to come again.

Bismilla Arathma Nerakeem.

Usman Shazad (11)
Pirton Hill Junior School, Luton

My Little Sister

My little sister is really funny,
Her favourite thing is money.
All she does is spend, spend, spend,
While breaking things mum has to mend.
My little sister is a really lively girl,
She also enjoys standing at the mirror doing a twirl.
Sometimes we shout at each other and scream
But when we are friends we are a good team.
I have a great sister, I know she feels the same
And at the end of the day we laugh and play games.

Megan Graham (11)
Pirton Hill Junior School, Luton

Wind

The wind travels north, east and west.
His powerful blow knocks my hat off.
When it's hot he lets off a breeze,
Helping me to cool down.
When it's cold, he gives me shivers down my spine
Which he passes by
And brings a little tear to my eye.
I'm happy when he's gone
So I can get warmed up again
By the sun.

Aisling Maynard (11)
Pirton Hill Junior School, Luton

Mum

You are like my best friend but closer
You are there when I need you most
You are like my heart but more precious
You are what my life needs to go on
You are my closest buddy
You're the piece of the jigsaw puzzle that creates me.

Thank you, Mum, for all you've done.

Nicole Baxter (10)
Pirton Hill Junior School, Luton

Little Twinkle

I think about you day and night,
Everyone says you glow so bright,
I wake up and see your sparkling light,
Little twinkle through the night,
You are the best above the rest,
You shine from east to west.

Abbie McSavaney (9)
Pirton Hill Junior School, Luton

Andy The Football Player

Andy went training
on Monday.
We did a few passes
and matched other classes.

Then a match on Tuesday
I took a shot
it went in the air
and past the whole lot.

Now a tournament on Wednesday
I played away.
I have lots of fun
and I had a good day.

Today is Champions League.
I think I did good
and played
as I should.

Shaquille Pessoa (10)
Pirton Hill Junior School, Luton

Euro 2004

We're off to Portugal vs France
They've got Henry, Viera, Zidane, no chance!

We might have Beckham but not Henry
They're both rich, they got no fee.

And all the decent teams, Germany, Italy,
Holland, Portugal the team host
Are we gonna win? There's nothing to boast!

Everyone's gonna bet England to win
After 2 matches we're out
The bet's in the bin!

Andrew Day (10)
Pirton Hill Junior School, Luton

School Time

You wake up on Monday
time for school
you wish you were on holiday
lying in a pool

You get up on Tuesday
time for a test
finally school's over
now I can rest.

You wake up on Wednesday
we'll have a good laugh
when I go home
I'll have a hot bath.

You get up on Thursday
time for break
and after school
I'm having a picnic.

You wake up on Friday
let's have some fun
school's nearly finished now
so I can go out and run.

David Way (10)
Pirton Hill Junior School, Luton

Swimming

S is for swimming up and down to 200 metres
W is for worry because you might drown
I is for inner pool, make sure you do a doggy paddle
M is might get an award
M is for missed 1 lap to 300 metres
I is for imagining sitting in the pool
N is for 'nice strokes' says the swimming teacher
G is for gained an invitation to collect an award.

Chelsea Smith (10)
Pirton Hill Junior School, Luton

Maybe

Maybe yes, maybe no
If it's no
I'll eat my toe
If it's yes
I'll be the best
If it's no
I'll lose this show
Think about it
Let me know
Is it yes or is it no?
Tell me now
Quick, quick, quick
Time's running out
Tick, tick, tick
This poem's gotta rhyme
But I ain't got time
I need to know
Maybe yes or maybe no
I talk a lot
I lose the plot
I'm going out
To the roundabout
This poem's near the end
So could you tell me
Please, my friend
There's something that I need to know
Maybe yes or maybe no?

Rikki-Ann Moore (9)
Pirton Hill Junior School, Luton

What Is My Name?

She is as beautiful
as a flower and
her skin as soft
as lovely white snow.

She has very long
blonde hair, it is
right down to her
toes.

She lives somewhere
nice in a very big
big castle.

Sleeping Beauty.

Anna Grant (10)
Pirton Hill Junior School, Luton

Feelings

I feel happy today,
Let's go out and play.

I feel sad today,
I'm staying in and won't play.

I feel cheerful tonight,
Tomorrow I'm flying my kite.

I feel angry tonight,
I tear up my kite.

How do you feel?

Leigh Spary (10)
Pirton Hill Junior School, Luton

Poor Cinderella

Cinderella, all dressed in rags,
Invited to the ball,
What a surprise she can't go,
She'll have to miss it all,
Cinderella, Cinderella, oh deary me,
Cleaning up the dishes,
Missing the ball and the prince,
Wishing she was there,
Hoping it will come true,
Suddenly she's in a golden dress,
It's not poor Cinderella now,
Cinderella is off to the ball.

Lauren Baxter (8)
Pirton Hill Junior School, Luton

Goldilocks Sneaks In

G oldilocks sneaks in the house
O ldest bear's porridge too hot,
L ittle bear's porridge just right!
D on't sit on that chair!
I thought it would break.
L uckily runs off when the bears return
O ut of the comfy bed
C hase her! Chase her!
K eep her in prison
S he's a burglar!

Dylan Som (8)
Pirton Hill Junior School, Luton

Goldilocks

G oldilocks passing by a little cottage
O n her own
L et herself in
D igging in the porridge
'I t tastes disgusting,' she said
L ooked for the chairs
O n her own
C ouldn't fit on any of them
K icked a fit
S he said, 'I'll try the beds.'

Alex Rhodes (7)
Pirton Hill Junior School, Luton

Goldilocks

G oldilocks is very naughty
O h, she's so cheeky!
L icking up everyone's porridge!
D arling, don't be so naughty.
I didn't mean to break the chair it
L ooked big enough!
O nly ate the porridge because I was hungry!
C urly blonde hair
K icking the bears down the stairs!
S he is very naughty.

Rosie Sheppard (8)
Pirton Hill Junior School, Luton

Forever Friends

We are forever friends,
Our friendship never ends,
We often argue
But nobody can split us up.
We are forever friends!

We are forever friends
Until our journey ends.
When we are apart,
It feels like they're breaking my heart.
We are forever friends!

Georgia Abbott (9)
Pirton Hill Junior School, Luton

Me And My Lion

My name is Ryan
I have a pet lion
He acts real tough
But he looks dead rough
With his mane that is scruffy
He'd even scare Buffy
With his big, fat belly
And his feet that are smelly
At night he eats meat while
He dances to the beat.

Ryan Hynes (10)
Pirton Hill Junior School, Luton

Lions

Lions are scary
I am wary
Fighting
Biting
Bashing away
Eating
Beating
All the meat is gone
The victim is gone forever.

Matthew Bonnar (8)
Pirton Hill Junior School, Luton

Birds

Birds come in all shapes and sizes
Big ones, small ones
Tall ones, short ones
Fat ones, thin ones.

Ospreys, buzzards, eagles
And a lot more.
Birds who prey and
Birds who are prey.

Miles Braithwaite (10)
Pirton Hill Junior School, Luton

Cats And Kittens

Cats, cats
Kittens, kittens
Are very sweet
To play with.
Cats, cats,
Kittens, kittens
Are very fun
To have.

Samantha Cooper (10)
Pirton Hill Junior School, Luton

I Used To Feel Safe, I Don't Now

When we came home,
At first we didn't see,
The TV had gone
And the statues weren't there.

The statues were Mum's favourite,
Represented each of us,
She was really upset,
I heard her crying.

I used to feel safe,
I don't now.

I couldn't get to sleep,
Scared they'd come back,
I slept with the light on,
Jumping at each sound.

I used to feel safe,
I don't now.

The police came round,
They brushed up fingerprints,
It made me nervous,
Would they catch them?

I used to feel safe,
I don't now.

Why did they pick us?
Do I know them?
I hoped the police would catch them
But they didn't.

I used to feel safe,
I don't now,
I never will.

Rosa Ellen (10)
Rickling CE Primary School, Saffron Walden

The Journey Of My Life

I was born into the world
And started my journey.

My first day at school
And I loved it.

My first boyfriend
Was wicked sweet.

The work days were a drag
But there was a guy I fancied.

My child means the
World to me.

I was nervous about my daughter Jill
Going to school without me.

Then I retired, I was a bit sad
But my friends had a party for me.

I went to New Zealand
And then Africa.

Sorry, I have to go, my train is waiting for
Me to go to Heaven . . .

Bethanie Martin (10)
Rickling CE Primary School, Saffron Walden

It's Christmas - Cinquains

Holly
And Christmas trees
Sherry and mince pies too
Stockings are hung on the chimney
For you.

Tinsel
And loud crackers
Presents under the tree
Massive turkeys on the table
I see.

Alice Woosey (10)
St Hilda's School, Westcliff-on-Sea

Mary I

Bloody, Bloody, Bloody Mary
She was a murderous villain
She killed the people of her land
Because of their religion.

Bloody, Bloody, Bloody Mary
This was tradition
To chop off people's heads
And become a terrible villain.

Bloody, Bloody, Bloody Mary
Was as mean as mean could be
She only thought of herself
And her own victory.

Bloody, Bloody, Bloody Mary
She was a Tudor queen
Her stepmother Anne said she would
Turn out to be terribly mean.

Arianne Bray (10)
St Hilda's School, Westcliff-on-Sea

Accident

All is calm as I cross the road to my farm
until *bang!*
The noise is as loud as the lion's roar
as I lay there still on the floor.
Dragons rush by me on four wheels
and I hear the echo of my own squeal.
I look down at myself from above
and I think of the people that I love.
What is happening? I say to myself
Then I remember what mother had said,
'Don't cross the road, stay in bed.'
I hadn't listened and now I am dead . . .

Verity Birdseye (11)
St Hilda's School, Westcliff-on-Sea

Time

I was in a hotel exploring a room
When I saw a portal leading to doom
I shut my eyes nice and tight
Alone and scared in the middle of the night
But too late, all at once it had sucked me in
When I looked around I was in a raucous din
It was very dark in this hellish place
I had to move at a snail's pace
Demons surrounding me shouting, 'Hee, hee, hee.'
I wished I was back in my home town Leigh-on-Sea
Some were red and orange, others black and white
Some purple and blue, bruised from many a fight
With a flash and a bang I was back in the room
And time hadn't changed in the portal of doom!

Anne Bullen (10)
St Hilda's School, Westcliff-on-Sea

In Heaven

He is there looking down on me
In the place where he belongs
I miss him so
It feels like my heart has stopped
Beating and growing
It feels like a hole has been drilled
In my heart
But at least I know
He will be happy
In Heaven.

Hannah Caller (11)
St Hilda's School, Westcliff-on-Sea

Lonely

I feel all alone
in a lowly world
she left a long time ago.
Why must we die?

In life we think about death.
Some people wish their
lives would end.
Why must we die?

I think of you night and day.
I hope not in vain.
I wish we were together.

Natasha Hughes (11)
St Hilda's School, Westcliff-on-Sea

The Sea

I splash about
The beating waves
They crash down really hard
I wait
The next wave comes
I push off
I can feel the wind
In my hair
It feels so fresh
The sea is fantastic
Come and join in.

Alice Pearsons (11)
St Hilda's School, Westcliff-on-Sea

I've Got The Bug!

I've got the chickenpox
Maybe I should call Dr Fox.
I feel very ill.
I really need a pill.
Look at my head!
I think I should go back to bed.
I got this thing in my tummy.
I really want my mummy!
I'm really bad,
I feel really sad.
My dad just says,
'Go to sleep!'
I was just beginning to weep.
I've got this thing inside
But I can't hide.
I feel like I'm rocking from side to side.

Victoria Dolman (9)
St Hilda's School, Westcliff-on-Sea

Friends Forever

You are such a good friend
We will be friends 'til the end
Thank you for being my friend.

You are so loyal
I think you are royal
Thank you for being my friend.

We always have fun
We play in the sun
I want to be friends forever.

Kate Kellythorn (10)
St Hilda's School, Westcliff-on-Sea

The Moon

The moon is a bright,
beautiful light bulb
turning on at night.

Shining ice-cold in the
dark night.
Circling so that the
same side of its
surface always faces
the Earth.

Sometimes it's a
quarter
sometimes
crescent.

Moonlit nights as calm as the sea.
new moon means
it's black as coal.

Laura Crockett (10)
St Hilda's School, Westcliff-on-Sea

School Is Fun

Mrs Claxton is Ellie's mum.
She is so much fun.
School dinners are yummy.
They go down your tummy.
Maths - *boooooo!*
English - *yahooooo!*
Saná's funny too.
When she makes her ice cream runny.
Teachers talking in the staffroom.
Maybe we are doomed.

Olivia Leeding (8)
St Hilda's School, Westcliff-on-Sea

Thunder

Crash, bang, boom
Thunder
How I hate it!
It makes me scared
It worries me so
I think it's something
That fell down
So don't let me hear
Thunder!

Lightning
Is like starlight
Bright
Yellow
Shocking
Sharp.

Elizabeth Medhurst (10)
St Hilda's School, Westcliff-on-Sea

My Headache

My mum said I had to stay in bed,
All because of my stupid head,
I stayed in bed and watched some telly,
Then my mum came up with a plate of jelly,
I think the flavour was honey, it was very scrummy,
I think it has already reached my tummy,
'Mum, my head, my head,
I think I can get out of bed,
I feel much better,
Look, Mum, I've got a get well letter.'

Summer Coysten-Gillard (9)
St Hilda's School, Westcliff-on-Sea

First Man On The Moon

I'll tell you a tale of a man and the moon,
His name is Neil Armstrong.
A leader of men!
What a man, oh, so strong!

One day in July many years gone,
A brave bunch of men went off to the moon.
The first to walk on the surface for long,
Was this man called Neil Armstrong.

I'll tell you a tale of a man and the moon,
His name is Neil Armstrong.
A leader of men!
What a man, oh, so strong!

The name of his craft was Apollo 11,
His other crew member was Aldrin.
Those brave, famous men of Apollo 11!
For them, on the moon must have felt like Heaven.

I'll tell you a tale of a man and the moon,
His name is Neil Armstrong.
A leader of men!
What a man, oh, so strong!

Those famous words uttered that day,
'One small step for man, one giant leap for mankind,'
Will be remembered always.
Oh, what a day!

Laura Hutchings (10)
St Hilda's School, Westcliff-on-Sea

The Titanic

I was told by a young man about the lost Titanic,
He said, 'Have you heard of the ship that was mighty
But hit an iceberg and sank?'
He told me about this ship that sailed across the ocean,
When that happened a lot of families and friends
Cried and mourned in emotion,
It rose out of the sea, the ship could not bend,
Once cracked there was no floatation,
My eyes were staring at this picture that flowed around in my head,
I fell from my chair to hear about those who drowned
And now are dead
This story tells me something, something I can't explain
But sad and lonely pictures floating in my brain,
Even though there's sadness that sadness will not last,
The reason is what's now is now, Titanic was in the past!

Alexis Norman (10)
St Hilda's School, Westcliff-on-Sea

Illnesses

I f you're ill have a sip of Coke.
L ie down if you have a bump on the head.
L ong bars of chocolate will help the chickenpox.
N o more pills but lollipops will help your tummy ache.
E very day you will have lice if you don't sit and watch a film.
S chool no more if you have a sore throat,
shh . . . be quiet or Mum will find out.
S uper bug I have got, go away or I will get cross.
E ggs I will have to cure my cold, if not I will go insane!
S leep, sleep all day long, no school, *yay!*

Rebecca Buckley Cox (9)
St Hilda's School, Westcliff-on-Sea

Illnesses

I'm ill, I'm ill
I need to go to the shop and get some pills.
But I've got to pay a bill.
Oh, I wish I wasn't ill.
What shall I do? There's nothing to do
When you're ill.
What have I got?
I think I've got the bug.
What shall I do?
I'm ill, I'm ill.
Now if I have the bug,
I must ring my mum for a hug.
Oh, but my mum's at work.
Oh, what shall I do?
I'm ill, I'm ill.
Shall I watch television?
No, there's nothing on
Only news
So what shall I do?
I'm ill, I'm ill.

Ella Henley (9)
St Hilda's School, Westcliff-on-Sea

My Diary

You're always there when I need to share
You're always there and you always will care
You're always there and you're always fair
And you can keep a secret anywhere.

I trust in you and you trust in me
Together we have a secret key
So I can open you when I feel sad
As writing in you makes me feel glad.

Camilla Smee (10)
St Hilda's School, Westcliff-on-Sea

Illnesses

Oh dear, oh dear, I'm ill
I should take a pill,
I think I've got chickenpox
Maybe I should go to Dr Fox.

Oh dear, oh dear, I'm ill
Maybe I could talk to Mr Bill
I'm getting cold
And I'm getting old.

Oh dear, oh dear, I'm ill
I will look how much money is in the till.
Ow! My head!
Maybe I should go to bed.

Oh dear, oh dear, I'm ill
Maybe I should call Lil.
I've got a bug.
Oh, look at that slug!

Samantha Hoar (9)
St Hilda's School, Westcliff-on-Sea

Teachers

Teachers are funny
Earn little money
They can be loving and caring
Put up with us moaning
'Stop whinging,' they say when our homework is lost
But most of the time they are happy and chatty
I think teachers are really batty.

Monique Turner (9)
St Hilda's School, Westcliff-on-Sea

Illnesses

Lying in bed watching TV
This is the life for me!
Broken bones and lots of groans
Sitting in a surgery.
The good things about illnesses
Are getting no school and no telling off for me!
Walk to school and break your leg
And bed is coming to me!
Oh no! Chickenpox, phone Doctor Box!
And he will come running to me.
Sneaking ice cream to my room,
Getting a major brain freeze.
Going back to school,
Fall off my chair and fake I'm dead!
Right in the middle of a spelling test.

Hope Ayers (9)
St Hilda's School, Westcliff-on-Sea

Char Jeffs

My best friend is called Char Jeffs
I do everything with her
She's bright, funny but sometimes dumsy
And her mum is Auntie Sharon
She's a great and trusting friend
She always keeps my secrets
And I know I am right to trust her
She lifts my spirits when I am down
She makes me smile if I have a frown
She's my best friend in the town.

Char Jeffs!

Francesca Bonomo (9)
St Hilda's School, Westcliff-on-Sea

Feeling Ill

If you've got a pain in your head,
You should lie down in bed.
If you have a broken bone,
I think you should moan and groan.
Oh, I had a cough, I need some medicine,
Quick, quick, turn on the television.
My eyes are sticking together, get my eye drops,
You've got conjunctivitis, you need some lollipops.
What are these spots on my face?
Chickenpox, I'll call Dr Race.
My nose is blocked,
It feels like a rock.
Boil some oil and place on head,
Head lice will be gone, just cuddle up to Ted.

Isobel Dudley (9)
St Hilda's School, Westcliff-on-Sea

Dr Pure

If you ever need a cure,
Just go and call Dr Pure.
From ill to pill,
From boil to oil,
You'll soon be in bed, in a coil.
He's made his own cures,
So if someone threw stones at your bones
And you've got the moans and groans
Or got a nasty, ghastly bug
Or even got the chickenpox
You just *might* call Dr Fox.
But if you've got some cuts and bruises
And if you're very old and cold
Or if you just need another cure,
Mum would say, 'Oh, please, just go and call Dr Pure.'

Lina Khazim (9)
St Hilda's School, Westcliff-on-Sea

My Illness

I once was ill and had to take a pill.
I wanted to go to school
To see my friends
But the doctor said
I have to stay at home instead
And sent me up to bed
And I was a sleepyhead.
In the morning my mum read me a story.
It was about Balamory.
It reminded me about the time
I wrote a story.
The next day I felt much better
And I heard my mum say,
'Here's your sweater.'
My sweater kept getting wetter and wetter
But the day kept getting
Better and better!

Coral Smith (9)
St Hilda's School, Westcliff-on-Sea

Mrs Claxton

Mrs Claxton is our teacher
And she really is fun.
She is Ellie's mum.
Mrs Claxton is really fair
On everything, really fair.
She has straight, blacky-brown hair.
Mrs Claxton is really funny.
She likes chocolate runny.
Mrs Claxton has a bunny.
She is funny.
Mrs Claxton is really nice.
She really likes rice.

Saná Chaudhry (7)
St Hilda's School, Westcliff-on-Sea

When I Had The Fever

A bucket would've been handy
Because I wasn't fine and dandy
Oh! And look! Oh! Yuk!
Out comes the muck
I'd been feeling kinda funny
It was all sloppy and runny
Then the doctor came in
And lifted up my chin
Then down it went again
Another shoot of pain
But out comes the nasty
Oh, I am feeling ghastly!
Of medicine I am not very fond
Why can't they wave a magic wand?
Just when you're better
You start to feel even wetter
They turn you black when you're feeling blue
Oh! It's horrid to have the flu
I am feeling just like filth
This is not my best state of health!
Oh no! I think I'm going to puke
Oh great! That's great, the doctor's not gonna look
Yeah! I'm feeling better now
If it wasn't the doctor I don't know how!

Hannah O'Riordan (8)
St Hilda's School, Westcliff-on-Sea

When I Was . . .

When I was one I played with a gun,
When I was two I first flew,
When I was three I climbed a tree,
When I was four I answered the door,
When I was five I made a beehive,
When I was six I played tricks,
When I was seven I went to Heaven.

Sammi Zelkin (10)
St Hilda's School, Westcliff-on-Sea

Illness

I am so dizzy,
What shall I do?
I am sick, I think I have got the flu.
I feel dizzy,
Shall I call my sister?
Oh no, she is busy.
My dizziness has gone,
Now I have chickenpox,
I think I'm covered in spots!
Argh! A sore throat.
Oh no, oh no, what shall I do?
Shall I mmm . . . take some medicine?
No, that is for sickness.
Oh yes, I shall take one tablet.
What shall I do?
I'm ill!

Harriet Birdseye (9)
St Hilda's School, Westcliff-on-Sea

Mrs Claxton

Mrs Claxton is my mum.
She is lots of fun.
Mrs Claxton is helpful.
She is cheerful.
She is beautiful.
Mrs Claxton is wonderful.
She is kind.
Mrs Claxton helps my mind.
Mrs Claxton calls us honey.
She is funny.
Mrs Claxton is . . .
Achoooo!

Ellie Claxton (7)
St Hilda's School, Westcliff-on-Sea

Teddy

Teddy, teddy in my beddy
You keep me warm and safe inside.
I fall in a puddle
Then I cuddle you so I'm happy and dry.

Teddy, teddy in my beddy
I make a cake to share it with you.
I find a clue to share with you
So everybody is happy inside.

Teddy, teddy in my beddy
Let's have a picnic
With sandwiches and cakes
And milkshakes.

Teddy, teddy in my beddy
I don't need to say anymore.
I think they get the point
I don't need any ointment.

Teddy, teddy you're always in my beddy.

Beatrix Bird (10)
St Hilda's School, Westcliff-on-Sea

Weddings

Roses,
Flowers for you,
Teddy bears with love hearts,
the celebration of weddings,
is here.
Bells ring,
love in the air,
walking down the aisle,
love each other forever,
love you.

Zerah Rajulawalla (11)
St Hilda's School, Westcliff-on-Sea

All About Mrs Claxton

Mrs Claxton is the best.
Better than all the rest.
She is quite funny
But the things she does are sunny.
Some teachers are annoying
But the others are quite enjoying.
In the staffroom the teachers chat
While we do some boring maths.

Aliah Ullah (8)
St Hilda's School, Westcliff-on-Sea

My Brother

My brother is so very old
he likes to wind me up
but sometimes when he's sweet
he calls me buttercup.

I think he might be strong
as karate is his hobby
but if I tickle him lots
he goes all sloppy.

Charlotte Burgess (9)
St Hilda's School, Westcliff-on-Sea

Love

Roses are red
Violets are blue
They make me happy
Coming from you.
I look at you
You look at me
You make me happy
It must ever be.

Rhabia Nabi (10)
St Hilda's School, Westcliff-on-Sea

School

At school I love doing Maths.
When we do yoga we take out the mats.
Sometimes people are unkind.
My grade 3 friends are kind.
Some people make me feel really happy.
My friends are so funny.
Mrs Claxton is fun.
In PE we run.
Tom is the school cat.
In the playground we play with a bat.
My school is the best.

Pari Shah (8)
St Hilda's School, Westcliff-on-Sea

Homeless People

When I go past the homeless people
They always smell
I saw a man sitting on the doorstep
All alone
He had tatty, ragged clothes
He had a dog to keep him company
But this needed feeding
Always starving for food
I saw a man playing an instrument
A man wrapped in newspaper
A man sleeping on the street
I saw a man who was smoking
I feel sorry for the homeless people
I am glad I am not one of them.

Naila Khan (10)
Sidegate Primary School, Ipswich

Being Homeless

People who live on the streets
Don't have to be lonely
Picking lots of newspapers
For their warmth and living
Having only money for a cup of tea
Living on the streets in cardboard boxes
Looking into bins to find something to eat
Carrying their clothes in children's buggies
Found on rubbish dumps
Some go and live in hostels
Some want to stay on the streets
Dying from hunger, trying to survive
Some play instruments
Some sell magazines
Some sit with their dogs and ask for money
They sleep on the benches
And some on the floor
This is how they live with their raggy clothes
Around the world there are lots of homeless people.

Gulcan Gurgen (10)
Sidegate Primary School, Ipswich

The Very Poor Man

An old man wrapped in paper
Eating the old McDonald's from the bins of Ipswich
Rummaging for a cigarette to blow away
Spending their money on drugs and beer
Getting drunk
They smell like a dustbin
They look like they have just rolled in a puddle.

Nick Dzundza (10)
Sidegate Primary School, Ipswich

In Need Of A Friend

A poor, weak lady in need of a friend,
Her clothes in rags without a care.
A poor, weak lady in need of a friend,
Playing a whistle with a faded blue cap.
A poor, weak lady in need of a friend,
Rummaging in bins for scraps of food.
A poor, weak lady in need of a friend,
Trying to smoke the last of a slimy cigarette.
A poor, weak lady in need of a friend,
Moving like a fox as she searches through rubbish.
A poor, weak lady in need of a friend,
Carrying her home in two worn-out bags.
A poor, weak lady in need of a friend,
Watching the world go by without her.

Sarah Booth (10)
Sidegate Primary School, Ipswich

My Homeless Life

I see people
Living their own lives like I did
I see people
In the streets of London
I see people
With their families like I don't have
I see people
An aeroplane flies over me on holiday
I see people
Trampling on top of me
I think
I realise
It's my old, boring life.

Laura Baldry (9)
Sidegate Primary School, Ipswich

There Sat An Old Man

There sat an old man
with dirty bits of newspaper all around him
watching the world go by
having nothing to eat so he's as thin as a pin.
There sat an old man
carrying the tin in his hands.
He's collecting little money
by selling elastic bands.
There sat an old man
trying to sleep on a bench
with a nasty, dirty face.
The hands were clenched.
There sat an old man
who goes through different weathers
of sun, snow and rain.
He doesn't have a house to go to.
That must be a pain.
There sat an old man,
he was such a sight.
He obviously broke up with his wife
because of a silly fight.
There sat an old man
in front of him was a pan.
He was probably collecting money
for a bottle of beer or a can.
There sat an old man
looking through the bin.
He found a tin of baked beans,
they were still in the tin.
There sat an old man
feeling very lonely.

Sophie Coote (10)
Sidegate Primary School, Ipswich

Poor, Homeless People

Walking in the streets
I see the hungry homeless people
Sleeping on benches under bridges
In the freezing cold
Asking for money and food
Rich people walking by
Ignoring them as they are dying with hunger
It's getting colder and starting to rain
There is no home for the homeless people
When the rich people are under their blankets
All they have is some old newspaper
Searching in the rubbish bin for food
All they have is mouldy bread
Rain is getting worse
Babies are crying with hunger and cold
You couldn't believe your eyes
They are dying.

Sruthi Margaret Tomy (9)
Sidegate Primary School, Ipswich

Homeless

I'm sitting on the wet streets alone
With no one to love, all on my own
I'm sitting on the wet streets alone
Feeling weary, cold and helpless
I'm sitting on the wet streets alone
Begging all on my own
I'm sitting on the wet streets alone
Feeling sad, ill and by myself.

I'm sitting on the wet streets alone
Newspaper as my warm cover
I'm sitting on the wet streets alone
Look like dirt, all alone
I'm sitting on the wet streets alone
    Help me, I say.

Rachel Healy (10)
Sidegate Primary School, Ipswich

Harry Potter

Harry Potter is the best,
He has beaten all the rest,
On his broomstick he flew high,
Right up into yonder deep blue sky,
With his wand he cast a spell,
But it let off quite an awful smell,
Had the wand been damaged in flight?
Was it because he was at such a height?
No, the truth must be known,
The wand had been tampered with by a naughty gnome,
Potter must have his revenge this day,
The gnome will have to pay,
Swooping low he sees the little green man,
And conjures up a wicked plan,
He raises his wand and fires a spell,
And turns his head into a ringing bell,
That will teach him a lesson for a day or two,
Unless he tampers with something new.

Tabby Hayman (9)
Sidegate Primary School, Ipswich

The Lives Of The Homeless

Knocking over trash to get food.
Only dogs for company.
Walking but nowhere to go.
Begging for money to keep alive.
Sleeping on grates to keep warm.
A dirty face and plaited hair.
Picking up the ends of cigarettes ready to smoke.
Picking at the 2p machines in hope of some money.
Sleeping under the bridge in a cardboard box.
If they can't sleep under the bridge they would walk.
Going in any dry place for shelter.

Stuart French (10)
Sidegate Primary School, Ipswich

Homeless And Sick

A lady, homeless and sick
Sitting there like a bag of potatoes
With matted hair, as smelly as a skunk.
A man, homeless and sick
No friends to talk to, playing the flute, trying to collect money.
A lady, homeless and sick
Laying peacefully on a grate
Keeping herself to herself.
A man, homeless and sick
Rummaging in bins for food, drinks and comfort
Living in boxes like rats and mice.
A lady, homeless and sick
Laying on a gravestone
With a cover of newspaper, sheltering from the cold rain.
A man, homeless and sick
Keeping a dog for comfort
Crying for sympathy
A lady, homeless and sick
Wearing all she owns
Her whole world in her plastic bag.
A man, homeless and sick
Begging for money
Throwing bottles at people.

Lisa Crane (10)
Sidegate Primary School, Ipswich

Cats

All cats are cute and cuddly,
Sometimes they can be annoying,
When they are hungry they miaow,
If they are happy they walk with you,
When they are cold they lay on your lap,
But when they sleep they purr with joy.

Sadie Fountain (9)
Sidegate Primary School, Ipswich

Street Man

The man who lives in the street.
A bin bag for a pillow.
Newspaper for a cover.
Rags for his clothes.
Toilet water for a wash.
As skinny as a stick.
A box for his house.
Watching the world go by.
Money is nothing.
Rubbish is his food.
Smelly, grubby is the man on the street.
His name is the street man.
He was once a man but now a tramp.
The town is his garden.
The air vent is his radiator.
    The street man.

Alex Quinton (10)
Sidegate Primary School, Ipswich

My Planet

If there was a place,
Floating around in space,

What a funny place it would be,
With people that could see,

The whole universe inside out,
But when they decided to go out and about,

They took a turn for the worse,
For when they caught a curse,

They went back, their place was destroyed,
But when they found a new place they were overjoyed!

Euan Connolly (10)
Sidegate Primary School, Ipswich

Don't Go There . . .

If there's a house,
In your neighbourhood,
That no one lives in,
Don't go there . . .

If you hear spooky noises,
In the night,
And they give you a fright,
Don't go there . . .

And if you're dared,
To sneak in one night,
And if it gives you nightmares,
Don't go there . . .

But . . .
Go there if . . .
You have a key!

Jessica Ellwood (10)
Sidegate Primary School, Ipswich

Homeless

His dog lies there all shabby,
He has forty-nine pence,
Buys some window cleaner,
Goes outside,
Downs the lot.
What else can he have?
He goes to a supermarket and nicks a trolley,
He uses it as a bed for the night.
What else can he have?
He finds a cigarette butt and lights it.
What else can he have?
He finds a sleeping bag covered in grime,
And falls asleep.
What else can he have?
What else can he have?

Frazier Seager (10)
Sidegate Primary School, Ipswich

On A Dark, Rainy Night

On a dark, rainy night,
Sat a hungry, lonely man.
His clothes were such a sight,
As he drank from a beer can.

On a dark, rainy night,
Sat a dirty, tatty girl.
Her dog gave people such a fright,
As she dreamed of a pearl.

On a dark, rainy night,
Sat a scruffy-looking boy.
He sat in the light,
As he talked to his friend Roy.

On a dark, rainy night,
Sat a ragged-clothed lady.
As she scratched her matted hair,
She cuddled her baby.

On a dark, rainy night,
Sat a group of men.
Sitting on a road,
Calling for money as loud as they can.

Rachel Jones (10)
Sidegate Primary School, Ipswich

The Insane Pain

There was an old lady from Spain,
She was an awful pain,
She flicked some meat,
Mixed with peat,
Oh, wasn't that lady insane?

Emily Steward (10)
Sidegate Primary School, Ipswich

Loneliness

Why does it always happen to me?
Why not somebody else?
Everyone has someone to play with
I only have myself.

Loneliness beats me up inside
Punch! Kick! Slap!
I'm beaten up into a heap
No one will help me with that.

I wish I had a friend
A new girl is coming next week
I hope we will get along
We will if she likes to peep.

I'm not lonely anymore
The new girl has come
She comes from China
Her name is Shilum.

Hannah Gee (10)
Sidegate Primary School, Ipswich

Whale Haiku

He swims for twelve miles,
That is when he takes a break,
Then he swims again.

Charlie King (10)
Sidegate Primary School, Ipswich

Shark Haiku

He lurks in the depths
Of the Pacific Ocean
Where he hunts for food.

Ben Wyness (10)
Sidegate Primary School, Ipswich

Wrapped In Newspaper

Wrapped in newspaper,
The man walks along.
Wrapped in newspaper,
Limping, homeless and hungry.
Wrapped in newspaper,
He sits underneath a bridge.
Wrapped in newspaper,
Using a bin bag for a bed.
Wrapped in newspaper,
Struggling to keep alive.
Wrapped in newspaper,
Rummaging through the bin.
Wrapped in newspaper,
Fighting his way past life.
Wrapped in newspaper,
Watching his life go by.

Jonathan Abbott (9)
Sidegate Primary School, Ipswich

Reading Yesterday's Newspaper

Go away
Leave me to sleep. A bench for a bed
Cos nowhere to go in this horrible life
I live and know. My beautiful style
Disappeared just like that.
A fireman earning £500
A week
Lost my job. They say I reek
I take a bath every week
Not enough.
Take one every day
So I lost my job
So go away.

Shannon Kennedy (9)
Sidegate Primary School, Ipswich

Homeless

Walking down the streets
Looking at the poor
Who are desperate for food
People dying of hunger
People searching for food
A man dying out in the streets
With nothing to eat or a penny at all.
No loving family or loving friends
Trying to get warm with winter coming soon.

They're so sick and poor
Rich people passing by
Ignoring the homeless
Wearing ragged clothes
All day long
Trying to get food out of the bin
Oh I miss my family
I wish I could see them again.

Mary De Guzman (10)
Sidegate Primary School, Ipswich

Homeless

H elpless old men
O h I wish I could help them
M oaning for money on the street
E ager for warmth and food
L azy and cold, need shelter from rain
E ating dirty food off the street
S cared at night with no one beside him
S kint after gambling his whole life.

Jake Brooks (10)
Sidegate Primary School, Ipswich

Walking Round The Streets

Inhaling up cigars and eating drugs and pills
Just sitting there paying no bills
And there are patches on my clothes and shoes
Watching my life go by, willing to die
Just want to sit there free
All I can see is bright things around
Begging for money, now that's not funny
A fist strikes once, then twice
They have nicked all my change

But now I'm nothing to many people
I'm just laying here watching cloud pass cloud
All that I have in two bags
I sleep in a cardboard box down the subway
I shuffle through bins and gather my lunch
That's my life.

Alex Hall (10)
Sidegate Primary School, Ipswich

What Kind Of Life Is That To Us?

Seeing homeless druggies picking up fags
Killing themselves.
Having a dog like a normal person would.
Playing an instrument, not getting much money.
Laying on benches, wrapped in newspaper.
Don't care what's going on around them.
Even reading last week's newspaper.
Feeding the pigeons, keeping them company
Wasting his food.
Finding pennies to buy a hot cuppa tea.
Drinking half empty bottles people have left.
What kind of life is that to us?

Ryan Booth (10)
Sidegate Primary School, Ipswich

The Streets Of London

She walks through the streets of London
Her tattered hair like rats' tails
Her whole world is in two carrier bags
Her eyes, like a candle, flickering and nearly blown out.

Begging for money to buy her a cup of tea
Scrabbling in a bin for food to eat
Everyone looks at her because she smells like a bin.

He sleeps on a bench wrapped up in newspaper
A bin bag full of rubbish for a pillow
A dog like white snow to keep him company through the night.

Hunting for cigarettes to smoke, or some drugs to make him ill
Or some alcohol to make him drunk and go mad
He plays a flute to make him smile
People stop and listen to the sweet sound
He has a round hat and asks for money
He hears a jingle
And he smiles again.

A policeman comes along and tells him to move
He just nods and goes
This is life on the streets of London.

Georgina Mitchell (10)
Sidegate Primary School, Ipswich

Phil And Lil

Phil and Lil went up the hill
To fetch a bag of sweeties
They ate too much
And then threw up
And burst into a million pieces.

Amie Paternoster (10)
Sidegate Primary School, Ipswich

My Same Old Life

As people walk past they look as if I'm not human
I rummage through the same old dustbin
I walk through the subway pushing the same old pram
I sit on the grates smelling the same old revolting smell
I smoke the same old cigar
I hate my same old life
I sleep in the same old cardboard box
I wear the same old ragged clothes
I hate the same old bench covered with newspaper
I want to not have the same old life
I have to feed the same old dog
I find the same old food
I wish I didn't have the same old life
I wish I didn't have the same old rubbish bag pillow
I play the same old guitar to my hopeless crowd
I beg for money to the same old people
I dream the same old dream
I wake up to the same old life
I hate my same old life.

Adele Hall (10)
Sidegate Primary School, Ipswich

Eagle

Tearing through the sky,
Finds prey to feed to their young,
With sharp beaks and claws.

Large and dangerous,
Hunts small birds, fish and rodents,
They are also rare.

Spreading out their wings,
The colours are mostly brown,
Birds of prey also.

Rebecca Gander (9)
Sundon Park Junior School, Luton

Cruelty To Animals

I hate it when people are cruel to animals
It is very, very sad
It makes me so mad
Why can't it stop?

When you see it done
Phone the RSPCA, they will come
If they don't, phone again
And they will say, 'OK then'
Why can't it stop?

If this poem won't stop it
What will help a bit?
What about the poor animals?
Why can't it stop?

Who is listening to me?
You know it's wrong, can't you see?
I hate it so much
So please, help to stop it.

Kymberly Chapman (9)
Sundon Park Junior School, Luton

Alphabet Poem

An antagonising aqua anteater answering
A bombastic beige baboon bellowing
A creepy crimson caterpillar crawling
A devilish damson dog decomposing
An evil emerald eel eating
A freaky frosty frog fencing
A growling grey goat grazing
A howling hazel horse hammering
An ill indigo imp inhaling
A jealous jet-black jackal jumping.

Ashé Elliott (8)
Sundon Park Junior School, Luton

The Snow Spider

The girl with a pale face
With the eyes that always like to glare
Her lips pale like a peach
Her hair so curly
Her nose so small
Her name is Bethan
Where did she go?

The boy with magical hands
With glaring eyes that are always there
Brown or black hair quite short
His hair so straight
His nose so small
His name is Gwyn
Why did he stay?

The spider with a snowy body
With small tentacles
Her eight thin legs
Her head so tiny
Her icicles so cold
Why did she go?

Laura Meehan (11)
Sundon Park Junior School, Luton

Alphabet Poem

(An extract A - E)

A nts and alligators are often annoying
B ouncing bananas bounced badly
C heerful chimpanzees chased cheeky children
D angerous dragons danced daintily
E lves eat eggs with elephant ears.

Samantha Fortune (9)
Sundon Park Junior School, Luton

The Lion

Muscles pumping like an exercise bike
The plains wide
The zebra zooms ahead
The lion pounces
And the zebra is dead
Fast and swift she had been
Slowly she licks herself clean

Suddenly there is a movement in the bushes
The tiniest of them all
But the lion's senses are sharp and she is no fool
She flies furious and wild
A shot is heard
And she slumps to the floor
The lion runs no more

Her eyes flicker open
Where is she?
She scans her surroundings
Where can she be?
The keeper enters the pen
And roaring can be heard

Fur now matted
Sluggish and slow
She is no longer fast
As seconds tick by
The lions starts to die
And now she is dead
Let us hope animals will be treated better
In the future ahead.

Elizabeth Butler (10)
Sundon Park Junior School, Luton

My Gran

My grandma's face is very soft like a petal on a flower.
My grandma's eyes are like sparkly jewels shining in the sun.
My grandma's hands are wrinkly but smooth.
My grandma's clothes are so beautifully decorated and she
wears a shawl on top.
My grandma is very straight. She may look weak but to me she's great.
I love my grandma and I'm sure she loves me too. I wish I could
go to her house more often.

Neha Shaida (9)
Sundon Park Junior School, Luton

Summer Acrostic

S ummer has come!
U seful bees help us make honey.
M ost people enjoy hot, delicious barbecues.
M any excited children splash in paddling pools.
E veryone goes sunbathing on the beach.
R eally wonderful summer!

Gareth Parles (9)
Sundon Park Junior School, Luton

Spring Acrostic

S pring is on its way!
P rimroses gloom on the grass.
R unners run in the cool wind.
I n the trees the robins sing.
N aked trees have got no leaves.
G reat wonderful spring!

Muhammad Sherrief (8)
Sundon Park Junior School, Luton

The Way I See War

The way I see war is
Terrifying tanks blowing things up
Heroic, brave soldiers fighting for our country
People being shot at, praying for their lives
The enemy messing up our lovely land and trees.

The way I see war is
Innocent people being shot and tortured in devastating ways
Soldiers being killed in front of little ones
People's houses being bombed and making people homeless
Were is the love in war? There is no love in war.

The way I see war is
Soldiers firing bullets anywhere
People screaming and dying of chemical gasses
Prisoners of war being gassed in gas chambers
I hate war, it's wrong! Wrong! Wrong!

Jack Price (10)
Sundon Park Junior School, Luton

The Silver Moon

The moon is as shiny as a fork,
It sees if you're about to talk,
The moon is as white as a plain sheet of paper,
The moon is like an eye spying on the world,
The moon makes the world light up and then the weary night fades,
The moon is as round as a beach ball,
A white face in the night,
Then later there is night, then streets go white,
The world goes bright, in the night there is light
In the morning there goes the night,
Suddenly! Daylight.

Then later the moon comes up,
There's the life cycle of day and night.

Danielle Farrugia (9)
Sundon Park Junior School, Luton

The Horse

Puffing like a pufferfish
The field so wide and open
Foals are all around
She snorts in pain, and neighs
Other mares look, young between their legs
A young is born

The first three years are fast and furious
Beatings, hunts, chases, you name it
A strong man appears
The young turns to run
Hooves pounding over the uneven ground
Muscles working like clockwork, mind reeling
The colt's delicate ears hear the sound of a gun
The colt lays like a lump of hay

Man upon his back, straps around him
Eyes dull and sunken
As his life draws to an end
People look and stare
As the day dawns, the horse lay lifeless and gone
On his grave is the name
Milton.

Jenna Kay (11)
Sundon Park Junior School, Luton

War

Sad,
    Sad,
        It's so sad,
            If there was only one way,
                That we could change the plans of today,
                    Sounds of planes crashing,
                        Sounds of weeping hearts dashing,
                            It's so sad.

Sarah Burnett (9)
Sundon Park Junior School, Luton

My Guinea Pigs

My guinea pigs are lovely to cuddle
They sometimes get in a really big muddle.
But hey, I still love them
They're like my little gem.

I let them in the garden when it's sunny
Also they can be very funny.
I've had my guinea pigs for about two years
And they have really floppy ears.

I would never give my guinea pigs away
I care for them each and every day.
My guinea pigs are getting chubby
A lot of the time they get quite grubby.

I put a cover over them at night
But then I take it off when it gets light.
My guinea pigs are always together
They will always be friends forever.

Bethany Cussen (9)
Sundon Park Junior School, Luton

Penguin Poem

The penguin awkwardly waddles across the ice,
Occasionally stopping to sight its surroundings.
But its awkward waddle soon turns into . . .
Remarkable grace and agility as she dives into the water.
Gracefully she slips through the water,
Hunting for her prey.
When satisfied with her amount of fish she returns
To land to feed her adorable young ones.

Victoria Banks (11)
Sundon Park Junior School, Luton

The Hedgehog

He follows his nose
Wherever it goes
Looking for delicious food.

Creeping, crawling hedgehog.

He is as prickly as a thorn bush
As small as a grapefruit.

Creeping, crawling hedgehog.

He comes out at night
After spending all day sleeping under a shrub.

His gleaming eyes look like twinkling
Stars in the night sky.

Creeping, crawling hedgehog.

Munching on earthworms
Millipedes and earwigs stroll across the
Garden wall
Looking out
Predators!

What a great
Hedgehog.

Solita Nanton (11)
Sundon Park Junior School, Luton

Alphabet Poem

(An extract A - E)

A wful astronaut arrowing at ants.
B egging bull bringing bad breath
C ockroach crunching chocolate cheddar cheese
D inosaurs digging disgusting dirt
E xtra electric eel eating elephants.

Jacob Foy (9)
Sundon Park Junior School, Luton

War

The weak are killing.
Death,
Everyone scared,
Sky full of bombs.
Tree's life blood leaking
Death
Death speaks
Help us to stop.

Ping Hei Chan (9)
Sundon Park Junior School, Luton

War

Human killer,
Gun shooter,
Building burner,
Peace destroyer,
Blood bringer,
Bomb thrower.

Haleema Mughees (9)
Sundon Park Junior School, Luton

Spring Acrostic

S ummer is just around the corner
P eople's personal time
R ain, there is no rain
I nteracting with nature
N o time to stay inside
G arden gnomes put outside.

James Reid (9)
Sundon Park Junior School, Luton

The Snake!

The snake is a magnificent creature,
 Long, sleek and slender,
He's very sensitive about his food,
 He likes his meat tender . . .

Writhing through the desert sands,
 Or in your nearest field,
It doesn't matter, his teeth are deadly,
 Many weapons does he yield . . .

His venom soars through the air,
 To destroy all opposition,
It's plain and simple really,
 Just like adding or subtraction.

It's all work for him, no play,
 It keeps on going, right through the day,
Until it turns to night, then he has his say,
 He leaps and strikes his innocent prey . . .

Jordan Spain (10)
Sundon Park Junior School, Luton

The Sparkling Moonlight

A button put onto
the big dark night
the shimmering light
only comes out at night.

Aroosa Raza (9)
Sundon Park Junior School, Luton

Dolphin Haiku

As the sun rises,
In the ocean dolphins ride,
Now summer is here.

Nicole Reid (8)
Sundon Park Junior School, Luton

Snow Spider

The girl's ghost-like face
glimmers in the darkness.
As her wavy, long hair
glows longingly.
Her glassy wide eyes stare
into the future.

The boy's shocked face turns
to the girl.
His glowing hand
glittering continuously.

The spider's glowing body
spinning shiny webs.
His legs glowing
one by one.
But where is he from?

Jade McParland (11)
Sundon Park Junior School, Luton

War

Death closing in.
Bombs flying through the air,
Friends get bombed as they're walking.
Postmen delivering death letters,
Flowers dancing to death.

Robert Taylor (10)
Sundon Park Junior School, Luton

War

Tanks are rumbling like a monster's roar
Birds singing to the tune of death
Bombs cracking like lives miles away
Children wondering if their fathers are coming home.

Brandon Bacchus (10)
Sundon Park Junior School, Luton

A Day's Diary As Mr Chimpanzee

The chimpanzee swings to and fro,
Amusing himself in his cage,
Moping around when he's tired,
Pulling silly faces when he's not!

Playfully fighting each other,
A big grin on their cheeky faces,
Their human-like hands grab each other,
In an amusing game of tag.

Their big beady eyes look up to you,
Looking all sweet and innocent,
Roundy ears sticking out,
Making them more irreverent than ever.

After a hard day's play,
The zoo keeper comes to say:
'*Bedtime!* Mr Chimp'
As he brings the small creature in for lock-up,
Goodnight!

Danielle Nealis (11)
Sundon Park Junior School, Luton

Wood Mouse

With its long curvy ears
It hears
A noise in the distance
It quickly tells the others
Quick, hide
The predator has gone
It searches for food
It finally reaches some food
But then a tiger hasn't had a meal yet
It runs and runs as fast
As its little feet can run
But it was no luck
The mouse was the tiger's meal.

Conor Chamberlain (10)
Sundon Park Junior School, Luton

The Scaredy Cat

The lion leaps with his tail in the air,
Communicating with the elephant, warning him,
Fight me if you dare.
As he poises his paws in a perfect position,
And the baby elephant says, 'Come on Dad, or pay my tuition!'
The elephant's tusks are as dirty as mud,
That's because the last time he fought,
He lost with a thud.
The lion is sweating with excitement and rage,
And he hopes he'll be sending these things in a cage.
'Ready, set, go!' the Mini Mes say
But it's way too late, the elephant ran away,
But he did say he would fight another day,
Oh yes, oh yes, he will fight another day.

Rebecca Patrick (11)
Sundon Park Junior School, Luton

Monkey

The monkey has its own surroundings,
Day after day it swings from tree to tree,
In the zoo it doesn't have a clue what people do,
If people's hands smell horrible it will refuse with a dribble.

It loves the grass and will never pass,
The sun is the weather it likes,
Sometimes it wishes it could ride a trike,
If it falls it won't cry at all,
It will just sit on a stool.

It likes to smell the grassy world,
Full of trees and flowers,
Then I'll bet the sun will set
And it's time to go to bed!

Megan McErlane (11)
Sundon Park Junior School, Luton

Everlasting Night

I lie in my bed in a dark, gloomy room,
A light from the sleeping night shines through.
I glare at the silver-cream moon,
My eyes fill with glitter,
Outside my delicate window
I see clouds dancing around in different sizes.
The warm breeze of the wind surrounds me with comfort.
It whispers in my ear
The clouds stop and make a large ocean
The moon is smudged and hidden beneath the clouds
The clouds form a Heaven above
Birds surround the sky with their flying.
The stars twinkle with gold and silver.
I hear her calling my name repeatedly
She is telling me her last words:
'You're not alone!'

Bjourdashe Henry (11)
Sundon Park Junior School, Luton

Dolphins

Some animals scream and shout,
Some laugh and roar,
But when it all comes down to it,
My favourite animals are dolphins,
Because they swim around in the sea,
And then they laugh, he, he, he.

I love its light grey, silky, shiny skin,
It's like a slug slithering and sliding,
It dives in the air with the water dripping off it,
If you go on holiday you might see them in shows,
Jumping through hoops and swimming in rows,
But nothing is better than when I rode on one,
It was called Softy because it was the nicest,
And sweetest one there.

Shona Richards (10)
Sundon Park Junior School, Luton

Snow Spider

The girl just stands there unconcerned.
The boy looks scared, frightened, worried.
The spider shimmers carelessly, not a fear in the world.

She's glowing all over her body, her wispy, white hair suggests
a magical, mysterious past.
Her face as pale as a sheet of paper, her eyes glistening a crystal,
deep blue.
She looks pale, ghost-like, almost like a fragile china doll.
Standing there gracefully.

He stands there scared, worried, alert.
Power surges through his body, especially his hands!
His face looks ready, ready to prepare for whatever it was
he was about to do.

The spider spins its web carefully as though absorbed deep within it.
Its magic makes her special, almost like she's a creature with a
fascinating past just waiting to be explored.

The girl just stands there unconcerned.
The boy looks scared, frightened, worried.
The spider shimmers carelessly, not a fear in the world.

Pippa Kate Standard (11)
Sundon Park Junior School, Luton

The Elephant

The elephant stamps very slowly through the jungle
It makes a very loud noise that sounds like a trumpet
Its big, long trunk is like a long, rough snake
Its body is so rough like a coconut with hairs all over it
The big elephant is a vegetarian even though it's fat.

Natalie Allan (11)
Sundon Park Junior School, Luton

Snow Spider

The girl as pretty as a flower,
Her eyes as fragile as the blue crystal sea,
Her lips a peachy colour, a friendly colour, but also ghost-like,
Her long, beautiful curls dangling down her pale face.
But what is she staring at?

The boy's lips are as red as a cherry.
There is light shining beautifully in his hands,
His eyes are as wide as circles,
But why?

The spider looks like a shaped ice cube,
With a hidden picture,
But what is that picture?
I'm curious to find out more!

Tanesha Powell (11)
Sundon Park Junior School, Luton

The Snow Spider

Icy cold in the wintry breeze,
Will get you down on your knees,
Glowing hairs and shiny legs,
It's the spider of the snow.

Ghost-like face and wispy hair,
Her ever-going ghost-like stare,
Bright blue and glassy eyes,
She is the girl of all the snow.

Frightened, scared, completely shocked,
It's not because he was mocked,
It's the girl, the spider, that is why,
Gwyn use your powers, don't ever give up.

Sanjay Pattani (11)
Sundon Park Junior School, Luton

The Tiger

The tiger roams the forest
Smelling out prey
From miles away
His keen sense of smell
Is working overtime
His nose, a triangular bridge
With two tunnels
Is smelling savoury
He goes in for the hunt
Like a ball from a cannon

The tiger roams the forest
Up high
Down low
With hunger in its eyes
Creeping, the tiger is
As sly as a fox
Silently searching for supper
It craves the taste of meat
The tiger is determined
To track down its prey

The tiger roams the forest
Listen to the left
Listen to the right
Hoping to hear its prey
Scuttling about
The tiger is
As silent as a mouse
He won't quit
Until he catches
Something succulent.

Victoria-Amina Dautovic (11)
Sundon Park Junior School, Luton

Flowers

I saw a flower in sunshine
The petals are lovely
I like the different colours
It makes me happy.

Laurence Foreman (10)
The Ashley School, Lowestoft

One, Two, Who Are You?

One, two, who are you?
Three, four, walk to the door
Five, six, do some tricks
Seven, eight, do some more.

Aimee Seaman (11)
The Ashley School, Lowestoft

Little Jimmy Green

Little Jimmy Green
Never could be seen
He slipped on a banana
And landed in the cream.

Connor Elsom (11)
The Ashley School, Lowestoft

Woof, Woof, Dog

Woof, woof, dog
Sitting on a log
In the thick, thick fog
Waiting for a frog.

Tristan Vander-Molen (11)
The Ashley School, Lowestoft

What Is Green?

Green is a leaf
Green is a forest
Green is a field
Green is an emerald
Green is the grass
Green is a frog
Green is the colour of cats' eyes.

Matthew Bryant (8)
The Iver Village Junior School, Iver

As . . .

As slippery as ice.
As slimy as a snail.
As white as a sheep.
As red as blood.
As blue as the sky.
As green as the grass.

Bethan Gerrish (8)
The Iver Village Junior School, Iver

What Is Green?

Green is a field of glossy grass
Green is feeling sick and running out of class
Green is a forest with tall trees
Green is a great big ball
And green is a leaf, tiny and light.

Rhys Phillips (9)
The Iver Village Junior School, Iver

A Winter Wonderland

Children play with my white, snowy skin,
I watch as their stockings go up with a pin.
I bring cold weather throughout the season,
Although I cannot find a reason.

I chase some animals into hibernation,
Just as the Queen is having her coronation.
Hot dinners are steaming on the table,
As the horses are sleeping in their stable.

I watch people put their wreath on the door,
Condensation on the window more and more.
Reindeer clatter on the roof,
I hear the sound of every hoof.

The kids scoop up at my face to make balls,
They throw it at each other as their mothers call.
I watch as a child puts away its bicycle,
As the tree forms its first silver icicle.

People light their nice warm fires,
As the children hand out the Christmas fliers.
On an icy road cars slip and slide,
Just like a spinning funfair ride.

Santa leaves in his full sleigh,
Galloping reindeer begin to neigh.
With Rudolph leading they pick up speed,
Santa smiles, 'He's doing his deed!'

I watch as the big day finally comes to me,
As all the presents go under the tree.
The excited children rip and tear,
To see their new cuddly bear.

Florence Miller (11)
The Iver Village Junior School, Iver

When I Was A Child . . .

When I was a child I thought . . .
Big fluffy clouds were dragons,
Small fluffy clouds were strange puzzle pieces,
Little wispy clouds were chalk smudges.

When I was a child I thought . . .
Big fluffy clouds were monsters,
Small fluffy clouds were pieces of popcorn,
Little wispy clouds were waves.

I never saw the clouds
I just saw what I wanted to see,
But now I see the clouds,
They're the clouds, just the clouds, only the clouds.

Rebecca Crone (8)
The Iver Village Junior School, Iver

The Alien

There was a green alien from Mars,
Who drove around in a car,
His disguise was poor,
So everyone saw,
This groovy green alien from Mars.

Amy White (10)
The Iver Village Junior School, Iver

Birds - Haiku

In bitter mornings
Voices heard in distant trees
Birds lay eggs in nests.

Leo Smith (10)
The Iver Village Junior School, Iver

What Is Green?

Green is grass
glossy and bright.
Green is feeling sick
when you've drunk too much Sprite.
Green are the woods
on a summer's day.
Green was a pound note
with which we used to pay.
Green is a stem
silky and lush.
Green is envy
when you start to blush.

Amandeep Dhaliwal (9)
The Iver Village Junior School, Iver

What Is Green?

Green is forest
leafy and tall.
Green is feeling sick
when you are full.
When you are envious
you can feel green.
Eating green vegetables
makes me feel really mean.

Claire Brooke (9)
The Iver Village Junior School, Iver

Golden

The golden sun shines in the day
Sliding across the meadows in May
The chocolate melts in the golden heat
Sizzling on a pan like meat.

Georgia Pomeroy (7)
The Iver Village Junior School, Iver

10 Things Under My Bed

A creepy black spider,
A red smelly sock,
A big African elephant,
A graveyard of woodlice,
A green Lego dragon with no head,
An old video game,
A dirty bird feather,
A scary daddy-long-legs hiding,
A rusty battery,
And a great Yu-Gi-Oh card.

Conor Cresswell (9)
The Iver Village Junior School, Iver

When I Was A Child

When I was a child
I thought big fluffy clouds were strawberry candyfloss
Little wispy clouds were waves on beaches
A grey cloud cover was a grey blanket
Big massive clouds were big, meat-eating dinosaurs

But now I know, they're only the clouds
Nothing but the clouds!

Rachael Couchman (9)
The Iver Village Junior School, Iver

What Is Black?

Black is a cat, sneaky at night.
Black is feeling angry when you have had a fight.
Black is when you die. Nothing but black.
Black is when you bruise your knee.
Black is when you get hurt in the eye.
Black is behind the moon in the night sky.
Black, black, black - saying I'll see you soon.

Hayley Green (9)
The Iver Village Junior School, Iver

Gold

Slowly, silently, now the sun
Walks into the day, bringing fun.
Pouring gold to light all she sees.
Golden fruit upon golden trees.
Golden beams on smiling faces
As children run their sports day races.
Warming and glowing the golden beams,
Melting and dripping our ice creams!
Golden flashes reflecting on paddling pools,
Glowing brightly on shiny white footballs.

Lauren Friend (8)
The Iver Village Junior School, Iver

What Is Blue?

Blue is the sea
Blue is the sky
Blue is a tear
Watering in your eye
Blue is the wind
Rattling through the trees
Blue is the colour of some cheese
Yuck! No more please!

Madison Doey (8)
The Iver Village Junior School, Iver

White

Silently the white snow floating down,
Settling on statues like a crown,
Covering roofs with a dust of white,
Glistening snowflakes dance in the light.
The old snowman feeling old,
Wrapped up warm against the cold.

Kelsey Rogers (8)
The Iver Village Junior School, Iver

If I Were . . .

If I were a kangaroo
I'd bounce around all day,
And bounce on the bed
In a very bouncy way.

And my mother couldn't tell me
It's a wicked thing to do,
Since she would be a kangaroo
She would do it too.

If I were a hippo
I'd get muddy all day,
And put mud everywhere
In a very messy way.

And my mother couldn't tell me
It was a wicked thing to do,
Since she would be a hippo
And she would do it too.

Daniel James Evangelista (8)
The Iver Village Junior School, Iver

Things I'd Do If It Weren't For Teachers

Chew bubblegum all day
Push people out the way
Bring pets in school
Throw eggs on the wall
Go look on Ebay
And have a little play
Go build a pool
And play football in the hall.

Anthony Bradbury (9)
The Iver Village Junior School, Iver

Into The Lair Of Baron Jagula

(Based on a poem by Brian Moses)

No light ever falls on the bushes and trees,
the flowers there are mostly diseased,
but I went there once for a dare.
I went into the lair of Baron Jagula,
past brambles that felt like knives,
past skulls with red eyes,
past roaring lions,
past a sleeping troll,
past diseased rats,
right up to the door of Baron Jagula's castle,
where I stopped and knocked

and the door swung open to reveal
the one-eyed, old face of Baron Jagula.
His breath stank and I shrank back,
then remembered why I'd come,
'Here's your newspaper.'

Rebecca Plummer (9)
The Iver Village Junior School, Iver

Silence Is . . .

Silence is the night before my birthday.
Silence is after I've been told off.
Silence is when you're trying to think.
Silence is a tiger waiting to pounce.
Silence is when you're watching your favourite TV programme.
Silence is first thing in the morning just as you wake up.
Silence is when you relax at night.
Silence is the night before Christmas Eve.

Bethany Ellison-Perrett (8)
The Iver Village Junior School, Iver

Things I'd Do If It Weren't For Teachers

I'd bring in a phone every day.
I'd swim in the pool in May.

I'd come in very late.
I'd have a food fight with your mate.

I'd write on the board.
I'd pray to your lord.

I'd draw on the wall.
I'd bring lots of balls.

I'd run around the school.
I'd be feeling cool.

I'd play cards with money.
I'd make a mess and be funny.

I'd run around the class.
I'd wear a mask.

Anjali Rajal (9)
The Iver Village Junior School, Iver

School

Miss Gray's our teacher
The head teacher's Mr Collis
We go to school to learn
The children are preparing for
Alice in Wonderland.

Whilst some are singing
Others are practising after school activities
Some are at home playing
And some are doing their homework
As for the rest, who knows.

Monday to Friday, day after day
Our plants are growing
And our minds are expanding.

Maxine Woollcott (9)
The Iver Village Junior School, Iver

The Thing

S omewhere deep, dark and dirty,
L ives a thing aged thirty,
I t has fangs of bright gold,
T hough its power untold,

W hen it roars at us it will leer,
A nd it makes us quiver in fear,
I t gets steamed up easily,
T hen it calls us measly,

S hould I shudder at its power?
T hough I could give it a flower,
R evenge is not possible,
I am very tossable,
K icking and struggling won't loosen its grip,
E ventually you will feel as small as a pip,

C lick of a twig will alert it
R eally at the end you will go drip, drip,
Y es or maybe not thirty!

Conor Pearson (10)
The Iver Village Junior School, Iver

The Wedding

The wedding was a disaster,
But the midnight party was a blaster.
Some people came with beer,
Others came with gin,
To make the party go with a swing.
Uncle Phil paid the bill.
The blushing bride nearly died!
With the groom shouting, 'No! No!
I cannot do it, as I'm in love with Miss Hewitt.'
She gasped and said, 'Goodness me!'
The bride said, 'Oh well, there are more fish in the sea!'

Daniel Parslow (10)
The Iver Village Junior School, Iver

The Dream

My dream is to play for Man U,
And to score a great goal or two,
When you see me
On the telly
You will be stunned.

Playing along Ronaldo,
Watch him go,
Then there's me
Micky D
The typical slow coach.

Michael De La Salle (11)
The Iver Village Junior School, Iver

Snowflakes

Snowflake falling gently down,
Twirling, whirling, it doesn't cause a frown.

Shimmering, shining, looking so grand,
But then it falls slowly to the ground.
Put out your hand and it will melt on your finger,
Quick as lightning (it doesn't like to linger!)

Maria Clark (10)
The Iver Village Junior School, Iver

The Spinner

There was a young spinner from Iver
Who was determined to bowl his first fiver
He turned up at Lord's
To thunderous applause
But was slogged to midwicket by Godiva.

Thomas Buggey (11)
The Iver Village Junior School, Iver

Sun

I am hot and yellow.
I make people feel happy.
I warm the earth.
I make you feel hot.
I melt ice cream and chocolate.

I am in the sky.
I give you light.
I am a star.
I make you want to go to the beach.

I blaze in the sky.
I go down at night
And come up at sunrise.
I am the sun.

Joshua Pennie (9)
The Iver Village Junior School, Iver

Locker Inspection

Pan P
Let's take a look -
What have we here?
A sleeping fairy
A bit of pixie dust
A silver, sharp dagger
And that's not all -
A golden hook
A green hat
Some toy crocodiles
Some of the lockers I've seen, Peter,
Yours is best!

Catherine McCaffery (8)
The Iver Village Junior School, Iver

Purple

Purple is my happiness,
Purple is a smile on my face,
Purple is my favourite colour,
Purple is my grooming kit for horses,
Purple is the colour of juicy grapes,
Purple is the colour of succulent plums,
Purple is the colour of the sunset behind trees,
Purple is the colour of my teddy,
Purple is the colour of Eeyore,
Purple is my soft unicorn,
Purple is the colour of my book,
Purple is the colour of my door,
Purple is the colour of my floor,
Purple is the colour of my flower,
Purple is my happiness.

Alexandria Haslett (11)
The Iver Village Junior School, Iver

Shingle Doodle Deedle Dye

Shingle doodle deedle dye
Shingle doodle deedle dye
What's that shinning in the sky?
Shingle doodle deedle dye
Shingle doodle deedle dye
Is it Pluto?
Is it Mars?
Is it Venus up in the sky?
Shingle doodle deedle dye
Shingle doodle deedle dye
Oh my wonder, it's a star
Shining star high up in the sky
Shingle doodle deedle dye
Shingle doodle deedle dye.

Manisha Matharu (10)
The Iver Village Junior School, Iver

Locker Inspection

Beckham D
Let's take a look -
What have we here?
A football
A green captain band
A fluffy towel
And that's not all
A cold drink
Shower gel
Some of the lockers I've seen, David,
Yours is best!

Ross Smith (8)
The Iver Village Junior School, Iver

If I Were . . .

If I were a snake
I'd rattle all day
And be very noisy
In a silly way
And my mother couldn't tell me
It's a wicked thing to do
As she would be a snake
And she would do it too!

Shaun Thomas (8)
The Iver Village Junior School, Iver

My Pool

I love my pool
it's nice and cool
especially on a hot day
it's 10 feet wide
and bubbly inside
and I don't like it any other way!

Heather Bainbridge (10)
The Iver Village Junior School, Iver

If I Were . . .

If I were a monkey
I'd climb furniture all day
And suck my thumb every minute
In a very funny way.

And my mother couldn't tell me
It's a wicked thing to do
Since she would be a monkey
And she would do it too.

If I were a frog
I'd jump on beds all day
And do back flips every second
In a very naughty way.

And my mother couldn't tell me
It's a wicked thing to do
Since she would be a frog
And she would do it too.

Oliver Powell (9)
The Iver Village Junior School, Iver

The Things I'd Do If It Weren't For Teachers

I'd climb up every wall.
I'd run around with a ball.
I'd wear a necklace every day.
I'd go and play
And bring a rat in two week days.

I'd draw on the table.
I'd tell a really scary fable.
I'd pull funny faces
And go to different places.

Ruth Canning (9)
The Iver Village Junior School, Iver

Ten Things In The Queen's Wardrobe

A purple sunhat
Some money as high as a mountain
A pink, fluffy spare pillow
A matching pink spare sheet
A palette of make-up from Debenhams
A white, silky glove
A brown, rotten false tooth
A beautiful, white dress
A golden, jewelled crown
A pale pink handbag!

Poonam Mistry (8)
The Iver Village Junior School, Iver

Things I'd Do If It Wasn't For Teachers

Make a duck pond in the hall.
Play squash against the wall.
Ring the bell all day long.
Play pillow fights, you can't be wrong.
Kick the football out the window.
At lunch eat chocolate.
Swing from the lights and drink Coca-Cola
Skateboard down the corridors.

Jordan Fitzgerald (8)
The Iver Village Junior School, Iver

Anger

Anger is when I'm on my motorbike and a kid crashes
right in front of me.
Anger is when my brother gets money and I don't.
Anger is when my motorbike blows up.
Anger is when my brother gets something and I don't.
Anger is when I do something and my dad doesn't respect it.

Jack Friell (9)
The Iver Village Junior School, Iver

Fairy Footsteps

Fairy footsteps are hard to see
You won't find them, nor will me.

If you see a shimmer in the sky
You're sure to have seen one close by!

Fairies blend in with their flowers
They even have their own dewdrop towers.

Fairies, fairies are so small
You'll never see them at all.

Fairies love to see you play,
They will watch you all through the day!

Laurel Tirone (10)
The Iver Village Junior School, Iver

What I'd Do If It Weren't For Teachers

Make a duck pond in the hall,
Play squash against the wall.
Ring the bell all day long,
Play pillow fight, you can't be wrong.
At lunch eat chocolate and drink Coca-Cola,
Swing from the doors.
Skateboard down the corridors,
Fight and swear at your friend.
Pencils, rulers, flick and bend.

Samuel Pinkney (7) & Jack (8)
The Iver Village Junior School, Iver

Things I'd Do If It Wasn't For Teachers

Make a duck pond in the hall.
Play squash against the wall.
Ring the bell all day long.
Play pillow fights, you can't be wrong.

Joshua Hearn (7)
The Iver Village Junior School, Iver

Red Is . . .

Red is a rose.
Red is a colour.
Red is blood.
Red is the sun.
Red is an angry feeling.
Red is your maths book.
Red is your skills book.
Red is the night sky.
Red is your lips.
Red is an upset feeling.

Andrew Christopher Lakins (8)
The Iver Village Junior School, Iver

White

White is soft
White is clouds
They sometimes make you cough
There was a white cat, it miaowed
White is cosy
White smells fresh
There was a white bird, it was very nosy
I drew on white paper, the picture was my best
I got it right, it was a test.

Elyse Rose Lane (8)
The Iver Village Junior School, Iver

Things I'd Do If It Weren't For Teachers

Have playtime all the day,
Say some things you aren't meant to say.
In the canteen have lots of food fights,
Be Spider-Man and climb on the lights.
Run around and play PS2s,
Go into the toilets and break all the loos.

Joe Harris (9)
The Iver Village Junior School, Iver

If I Was A . . .

If I was a tiger
I'd go and kill someone
And if my mum tells me
It is a wicked thing to do
Well, she will do it too.

If I was a dragon
I'd go and burn someone
And if my mum tells me
It is a wicked thing to do
Well, she will do it too.

If I was an earwig
I'd go into people's ears
And if my mum tells me
It is a wicked thing to do
Well, she will do it too.

Shannon Kenny (9)
The Iver Village Junior School, Iver

Locker Inspection

Parker P
Let's take a look
What have we here?
A spider's web
A black spider
A mask
A wrestling outfit
And that's not all -
A pair of red gloves
A baddie tracer
Of all the lockers I've seen
Peter, yours is best.

Gino Stevens (9)
The Iver Village Junior School, Iver

If I Were . . .

If I were a pig
I'd grunt around all day
And splash in the mud
In a very rude way
And my mother couldn't tell me
It's a wicked thing to do
Since she would be a pig
And she would do it too.

If I were a tiger
I'd sit around all day
And eat all the things I see
In a very horrid way
And my mother couldn't tell me
It's a wicked thing to do
Since she would be a tiger
And she would do it too.

Natalie Stoker Baker (8)
The Iver Village Junior School, Iver

Locker Inspection

Crust J
Let's take a look
What have we here?
A juggling ball
A wig
A unicycle
And that's not all -
A bucket of water
A rope
Some red noses
Of all the lockers I've seen Joey
Yours is the best!

Emily Plaskett (9)
The Iver Village Junior School, Iver

If I Were . . .

If I were a lion
I would kill children all day
And make sure I ate them all
In a very vicious way.
And my mother couldn't tell me
It's a wicked thing to do
Since she would be a lion
And she would do it too.

If I were a parrot
I would swear all day
And copy everybody else
In a very delightful way
And my mother couldn't tell me
It's a wicked thing to do
Since she would be a parrot
And she would do it too.

Chelsea Nicholls (8)
The Iver Village Junior School, Iver

Locker Inspection

Let's take a look -
What have we here?
A club
An animal skin shirt
A baby dinosaur
And that's not all -
A giant rock
A pair of big, black boots
And some meat from an animal
Of all the lockers I've seen Fury
Yours is the best!

Edward Howes (8)
The Iver Village Junior School, Iver

The Club

Is a
Sweet-eating
Team-beating
Record-breaking
Loud-talking
Bat-hitting
Net-flapping
Umpire-shouting
String-pinging
Kind of team!

Rebecca Hiscock (9)
The Iver Village Junior School, Iver

If I Were . . .

If I were a monkey
I'd jump around all day
And bang my tummy
In a very silly way
And my mother couldn't tell me
It's a wicked thing to do
Since she would be a monkey
And she would do it too.

Charlotte Wade (8)
The Iver Village Junior School, Iver

The Man From Iver

There was a young man from Iver
Who was a magnificent driver
He forgot to brake
Ended up in a lake
And was rescued by a deep-sea diver.

Lauren Gibney (9)
The Iver Village Junior School, Iver

I Wish I Could . . .

I wish I could reach the sky
I wish it was not too high
I wish I could always die
So I could go to the sky
High above the clouds
High above my town
High above the ground
Where I never go down
But I'll miss out on Mum's lovely roast
I'd miss out the most
I wish I could not reach the sky
I wish it was too high.

Lucy Mitchell (8)
The Iver Village Junior School, Iver

The Street Car From Hell

There was a street car from Hell
That accelerates as fast as a gazelle
It has an exhaust the size of a rocket
And it's got a navigator the size of my pocket
It has a bottle of nitrous
With a garage the size of a fortress.

James Corcoran (11)
The Iver Village Junior School, Iver

Hole In His Hand

There once was a man called Queensland
Who liked to walk on the sand
As he started to dream
He heard himself scream
He had a hole in his hand.

Molly Green (11)
The Iver Village Junior School, Iver

The Rich Man

There once was a man
Who ate lots of ham
He had a giant house
With a big fat mouse
The more his house cost
The more he got lost
There were two ways to get upstairs
And he found lots of pears
He was so jolly
He married Molly.

Alexander Oaten (10)
The Iver Village Junior School, Iver

I Wish - Cinquain

I wish
I could be rich
And have a lot of games
And have all the games I want now
Have fun.

Bradley Ward (10)
The Iver Village Junior School, Iver

Camper Jake

There once was a camper called Jake
Who found a huge pin in his cake
He cut it in half
Gave half to the path
And then put the other half to shake.

Katie-Rose Sutton (10)
The Iver Village Junior School, Iver

Winter

I am winter
Cold, frosty, icy, snow,
Ice-skating over frozen lakes
Building snowmen everywhere
Wrap up warm and have some fun
When the blizzard starts run inside
Toasted marshmallows and hot chocolate
Are waiting by the fire
Christmas shopping, presents to buy
Decorating Christmas trees
Christmas dinner, playing games
New year is on its way.

Emily Faulkner (10)
The Iver Village Junior School, Iver

Riddle

He lives in a swamp
He's green and thin
He has sharp teeth
He loves to eat meat
With his big, bold eyes
But he doesn't eat flies.

Answer: Crocodile.

Luke Palmer (10)
The Iver Village Junior School, Iver

I Wish - Cinquain

I wish
Chelsea would win
Against Arsenal 10-0
It would be a great happening
For me.

Tom Urquhart (11)
The Iver Village Junior School, Iver

Dream

I had a dream
That glittered and shone
It always gleamed
In the bright moonlight.

A fairy I see
Riding a bee
The dream has gone
In the morn!

Huensa Mumin (10)
The Iver Village Junior School, Iver

The Perfect Shot

There was a small child in our school
Who always liked to play football;
His name was Scott
He had a perfect shot
And was always in space for the ball.

Robert Orr (10)
The Iver Village Junior School, Iver

The Fat Man From Iver

There was a fat man from Iver
Who was a professional diver
He got to the top
And then did a bellyflop
And won a big fat fiver.

Amber Willmott (11)
The Iver Village Junior School, Iver

I Won't Eat That!

There once was a boy who was sure
That he would not eat any more
Than sprouts and peas
And juicy cherries
Would there ever be a cure?

But one day the boy played dead
And his brother laid crisps on his head
He licked them up quickly
Didn't think they were sickly
And shouted and screamed till he was fed.

There once was a boy who was sure
That he would not eat any more
But he found he was wrong
And wrote this whole song
And now he eats anything but manure!

Sophie Jansz (10)
The Iver Village Junior School, Iver

Snow

You make snowmen with me
I hate the sun because he melts me
I am soft and white
I am freezing cold
I only come out in wintertime
You leave footprints in me
I have a best friend called ice
I cover things in white softness
When I am trod on I crunch
I entertain children and adults
You always play snowball fights with me
And you sled on me
I am snow.

Kyle Barnes (10)
The Iver Village Junior School, Iver

The Vicar From Spain

There once was a vicar from Spain
Whose manners at the table were a pain
It wasn't the mood
As he ate his food
But the way that he sat on his chain.

Michael Kessler (10)
The Iver Village Junior School, Iver

What Is . . . The Moon?

The moon is a white CD
Playing cheerful music.

It is a peeled apple
Quickly being bitten.

It is a white football
Being kicked into its goal.

It is a small, round lid top
Being unscrewed from its bottle.

It is a browny-white onion
Making people cry.

It is a drop of clean milk
On a dark, old table.

It is a white button,
Falling off a jacket.

It is a wet snowball
Being thrown in the inky sky.

It is a balloon
Flying into the deep, orange sunset.

It is a round, white rubber
Rubbing out mistakes in the world.

Roxanne Wauchope (10)
The Leverton Junior School, Waltham Abbey

Football

Football is cool,
Especially when winning football,
Scoring a goal is fantastic,
Clearly their goalie wasn't elastic.

Our goalie is brill,
Because he's got a lot of skill,
The defence is good,
While the coach says tackle if you could.

The midfield are stars,
Some can run at the speed of cars,
Our strikers are fast and weave about,
The ball hits the back of the net and we all shout,
'Goal!'

Darrell Duhy (11)
The Leverton Junior School, Waltham Abbey

The Blitz

The troops march down the city street,
Bombs exploded at their feet,
Buildings crumbling before their faces,
Roaring flames having races.

Children saying goodbye to mothers,
Getting on the trains with all the others,
Taken to the countryside safe and sound,
The others left at poor London town.

Fathers leaving, mothers crying,
Overhead the planes are flying,
Sirens wailing, bombs blasting,
Is this war everlasting?

Samantha Trott (10)
The Leverton Junior School, Waltham Abbey

My Friend Jake

My friend Jake
Came from a nearby lake
He swims so quick
And with just one flick
He is halfway down the lake.

He scared away all the boats
Without using a float
When he was at the end
He was ready for his best friend
To give him a hug or two
And then he caught the flu
Because the water was too cold.

Then he showed me how to fold
A paper star into three
Then he gave me some tea
With a slice of cake
And then he pushed me into the lake
Without my best friend Jake.

Sophie Canty (11)
The Leverton Junior School, Waltham Abbey

All About Me

I love my music
And I love to dance
My name is Mollie
And I've got three cats
I play the piano
With my friend Gaby
I support Arsenal
That's the team for me.

Mollie Warden (9)
The Leverton Junior School, Waltham Abbey

Sex Education Poem

Sex education is so rude
We see cartoon characters that are nude
Sex ed is just vile
It's not our style, but it does make us smile
The teachers try to keep a straight face
They do really wanna laugh, that's the case
Sex education is before lunch
It makes us feel sick, we don't want to munch
Why can't we do it just a bit before
Or we won't want to do it anymore
Some people can't stop fiddling
While others can't stop giggling
We work in partners, it's a team
The videos make us want to scream
I'm a schoolkid, get me out of here!

Matthew Cross (11)
The Leverton Junior School, Waltham Abbey

Playground

I'm always unhappy when playtime ends,
The lessons start and history begins.
And it's so unfair
There's no equipment out there
It's so hot
There's not enough shady spots.

When I get my tuck
I love eating it so much
I play with my friends
Until the playtime ends
And this boy at school
Thinks he's so cool
But he's actually a fool.

Danielle Dolling (11)
The Leverton Junior School, Waltham Abbey

Bullying

Bullying is nasty
Bullying is bad
After you've been bullied
It makes you a bit sad.

Bullies think it's fun
But really they know it's silly
But Billy the bully looked really silly
After he'd been punched on the nose.

The bully cries
And says his goodbyes
But really bullying is nasty
And bullying is bad.

Sam Starkey (10)
The Leverton Junior School, Waltham Abbey

Home Time

Home time man
It's really cool
Grab your bag
And run out of school.

Race down the corridor
Through the hall
Bouncing up and down
Forgetting about those rubbish rules.

Down the path I go
Racing to the finish line
Like it's an Olympic show.

Oliver Jones (11)
The Leverton Junior School, Waltham Abbey

Tests

Today we're doing a very hard test
I'm gonna try to do my very, very best.
First we've got maths and science too,
These are my very worst subjects to do.

Two plus two is four,
I really don't want to do any more.
The clock's ticking as fast as it can,
I'm sitting next to big, fat Dan.

He's really dumb
Now he's sucking his thumb.
I've been told not to cheat
My heart's pounding, I can feel the beat.

The test's nearly over,
I wish I'd brought my lucky clover
Ding, ding, ding, the bell's gone for break
I'm glad I brought my juicy steak.

Charlotte Chuck (10)
The Leverton Junior School, Waltham Abbey

Playground

I walk along the path
Playing football on one half
On the rock-hard ground
Seeing kids getting a pound
I'm buying old tuck
As I see the new delivery truck.

I scored inside the net
I won the 50p bet
Outside playing football
All the other classes waiting in the hall.

Judd Green (11)
The Leverton Junior School, Waltham Abbey

Teachers

Why do teachers even bother?
They're really bossy like my mother,
They bore us to death,
Who even cares about Macbeth?

The most boring lesson has to be,
RE or history,
But when Miss Medland teaches it,
We feel like we are part of it.

When assemblies come to mind,
Teachers really aren't that kind,
They say, 'Let's talk about the Jubilee,'
I'd rather do some numeracy.

Overall teachers aren't that cool,
But they are the main part of our school!

Shenice Harman (11)
The Leverton Junior School, Waltham Abbey

Tests

Tests! I hate tests!
Spelling test, reading test, they're all the same
Listen to me, tests are not my game
The clock ticks very slow
I wish I could get up and go!

Your hands begin to ache and ache
I would rather jump into a lake
Yes, the bell has gone, I can go home
Now I can sit in front of the TV with an ice cream cone.

I've got to get this off my chest
Tomorrow I have got a writing test!

Nicole Burns (11)
The Leverton Junior School, Waltham Abbey

Cinderella

Have you heard of Cinderella?
Yes, the one dressed in yella
She lives with her evil sisters and stepmother
They all hated each other!
There was a grand ball
In the prince's big hall
But she couldn't go, instead stayed at home
She sat there crying all alone
And then the fairy godmother came
She helped Cinderella from her shame
She got a beautiful dress and did her hair
Her shoes shone against her skin so fair.
She was sent away in her carriage so bright
When she got there she was filled with delight!
She was swept away off her feet
For it was the handsome prince she did meet
She forgot the godmother's wish
She was to be back at 12 within a kiss
She ran off through the doors
Then she lost her shoe to the floor
The prince searched every house
He even looked upon the mouse
In search for the girl he danced with
He could find and live
When he came to Cinderella's Mack
The smell told him he was on the right rack.
He knocked at the door
And stared at the floor
Out came the beautiful Cinderella
Yes, the one dressed in yella
She tried the shoe on with a hit
And yes, it did fit!
She was sent away in her carriage
To start off her marriage
She sent away her sisters and stepmother very gladly
For treating her so badly
The party was filled with joy and laughter
Everyone lived happily ever after!

Harriet Baker (11)
The Leverton Junior School, Waltham Abbey

A Faraway Place

One day I woke up in a faraway place,
Then I realised I was up in space

I looked at all kinds of funny things,
I hastily thought of school and how the choir sings

But after a while I got it out of my mind,
I looked around to see what I could find,

Then I saw something weird, at first I thought I was insane,
I stared at an elephant with a colossal mane

And a purple lion eating bananas and flowers,
I walked for hours and hours,

I found a house to sleep in for the very dark night,
The next day it was a totally different sight,

I thought they had no aviation or locomotion,
(Wrong) I saw a plane on tracks and a train flying across the ocean,

I went on spacecraft to another planet to see what was around,
I saw a beast I thought it was going to bite me I made no sound,

I ran to the spacecraft and went back, when I got there I had dinner,
I entered a race I ran like lightning, I was the winner

I thought about my home I liked it here so I went to sleep
I woke up at 4 o'clock, I woke up early because my alarm clock
went *beep*

I had chicken and snails, I didn't like it but I had to eat it so I did
The monster I saw on the other planet was here so I ran away and hid

I met an alien who was very nice, funny and popular, his name was Lee
He took me places that were brilliant I couldn't believe what I could see

I said goodbye to my friend, I got in the spaceship it was time to go
After a while I got home I got grounded for four weeks in a row

I got grounded, for the spaceship in the backyard
And because I went for so long, I got hit hard.

Lenny Baker (9)
The Leverton Junior School, Waltham Abbey

Making Shadows

Making shadows in the darkest places
These creatures of evil deny all faces
Invisible to the naked eye
The devilish minions creep swiftly by.

They hide in the shadows in grief and despair
Then they regroup and return to their lair
There an evil man stood
His evil face covered by his hood.

Then a foul voice crept through his teeth
'There is one man who can see you, his name is Hethaldeeth,
I want this man dead
And if you can, bring me his head.'

The darkness draped creatures for hours were seeking
And did not notice the morning birds squeaking
And the sun turned them to stone
And still to this present day you can hear them moan.

Duncan McEwan (10)
The Leverton Junior School, Waltham Abbey

The Dragon Woke Up After A Long Sleep

He yawned, showing his big, long, sharp, pointed teeth.
His tummy growled as loud as thunder, it was time to eat
He rose from his bed and stretched his wings
With one big jump he started to fly
Looking down he saw a big, fat, juicy sheep
Without any sound he swooped down
Swallowing the sheep in one bite
Then he went back to his cave in peace.

Danielle Stocks (9)
The Westborough Primary School And Nursery, Westcliff-on-Sea

The Spinner

On a cold, frosty night
I got a bit of a
Fright
Up in the corner
Of the room
There was a
Shimmer of silver
As I got closer
It looked a bit
Clearer
To my astonishment
It was a tiny spider
I ran downstairs
I found a fly swatter
So I grabbed it
I ran upstairs
I ran over
To the spider
I whacked it hard
I felt so guilty
I thought to myself
What have I done?

Jordan Giller (8)
The Westborough Primary School And Nursery, Westcliff-on-Sea

The Day At The Seaside

Once every year I go to the seaside.
The sea blows like the wind
It feels like I'm in the clouds
It's so smooth.
The water goes in my eye
It's so bright that my eyes go blue
The only thing that glows in my eye
Is the sea.

Farhana Khan (9)
The Westborough Primary School And Nursery, Westcliff-on-Sea

The Secret Illness

Friday night, I heard crying outside my door.
My mum was crying on her bed.
Whispers and private talks became a habit.
I started to get worried.
One day I had had quite enough
So I asked the question
My grandad was in hospital
He had had a heart attack at work
I felt so scared and had so many questions to ask
But knowing does not stop the whispering.

Emily Hawkyard (9)
The Westborough Primary School And Nursery, Westcliff-on-Sea

The Girl Of Winter

When autumn dies, winter's alive,
She brings a blanket of snow over the world.
She swoops across everyone bringing a chill of the wind,
She paints mountains on your windows with her icy nails.
If you're naughty she swoops across your door
And locks you in with ice.

Abigail Ridley (9)
The Westborough Primary School And Nursery, Westcliff-on-Sea

Normal

Why can't I just be a normal kid?
Who plays football and has a girlfriend
And have a mind that doesn't bend around rapping
Why can't I stop flapping my gums
But when a battle comes
My head is a stove top
It gets so hot
My mouth overloads with acid
I need to be like a river that's placid.

Nelson Bridgford (10)
The Westborough Primary School And Nursery, Westcliff-on-Sea

Sea

What can you see
Down in the sea?
Can you see me?

Can you see stones
Or ancient fish bones
Or bits of old phones?
Can you see ice cream cones?

Can you see a fish
Or a bit of old dish?
Is that what you wish to see
At the sea?

Hollian Gibbs-Leake (8)
The Westborough Primary School And Nursery, Westcliff-on-Sea

Monkeys

I think monkeys are funky,
They like to swing and play,
They like to eat bananas,
They like to climb trees each day.
I think monkeys are cheeky,
They always make me laugh,
They scream so loud, they make me deaf,
They make a mess in the bath.
I think monkeys are mischievous,
They always mess about,
But I would love one for a pet,
Even if it made Mum shout.

Melodie Webb (9)
The Westborough Primary School And Nursery, Westcliff-on-Sea